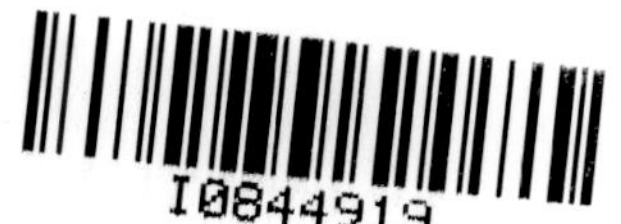

This Book Belongs to:

____

Test Color Page

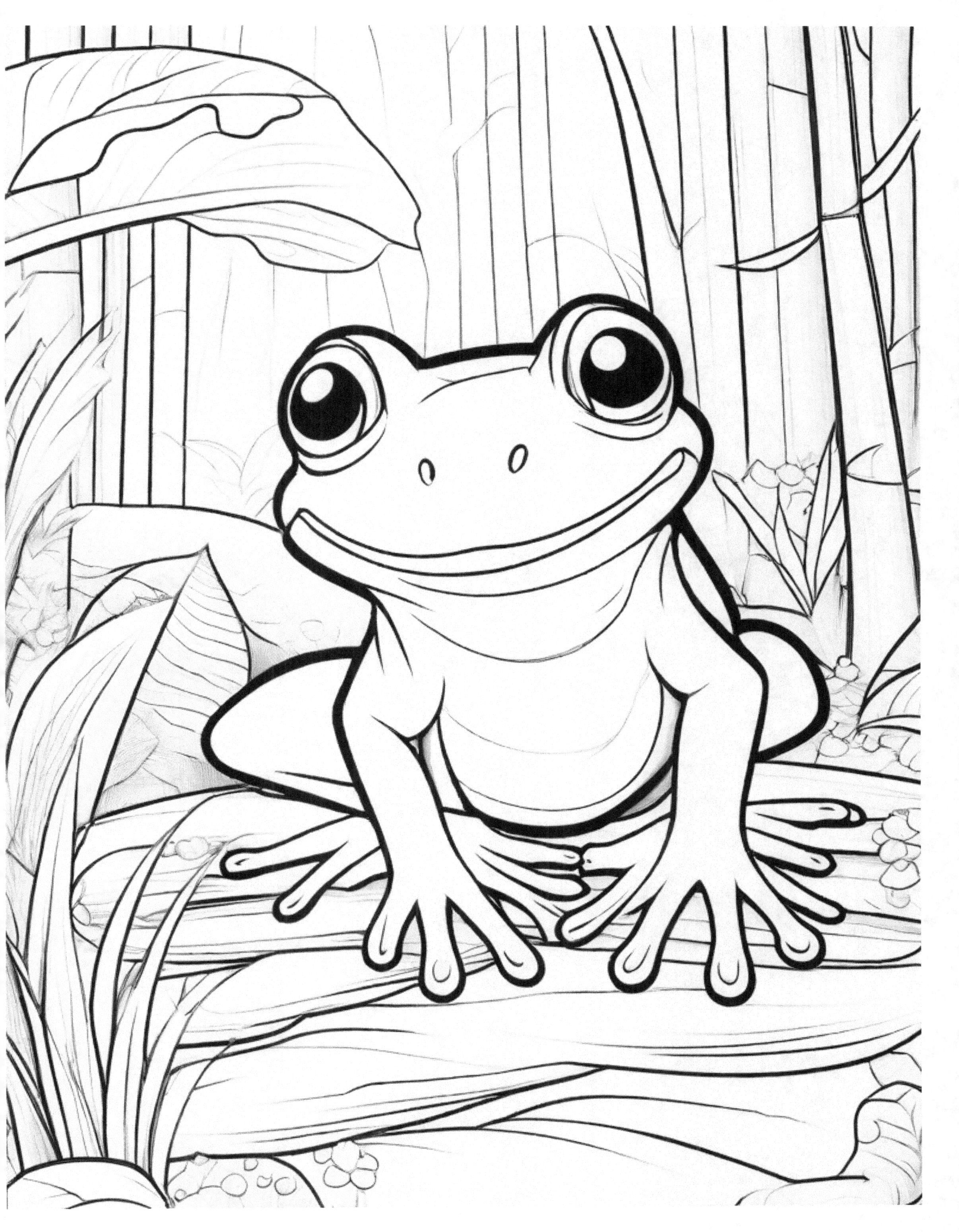

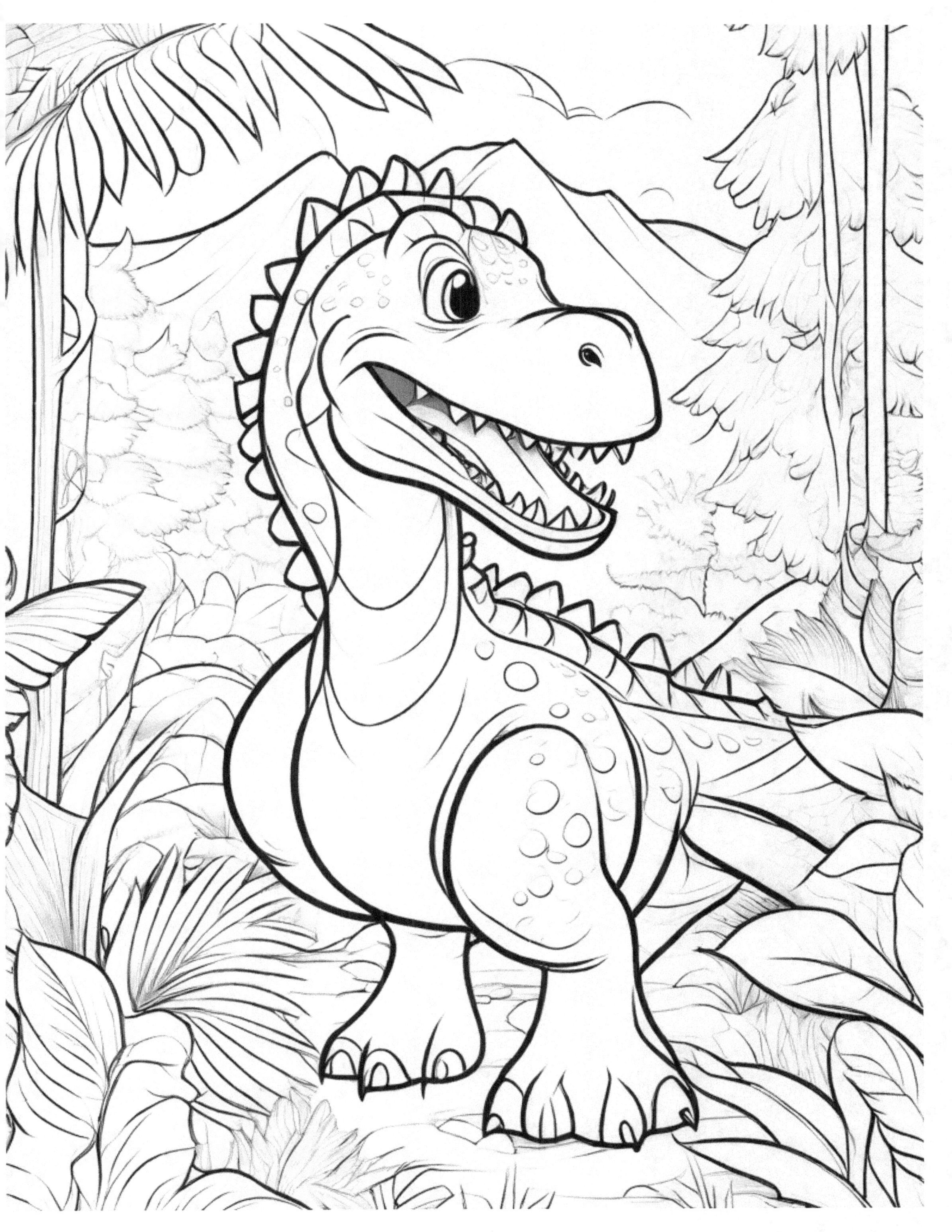

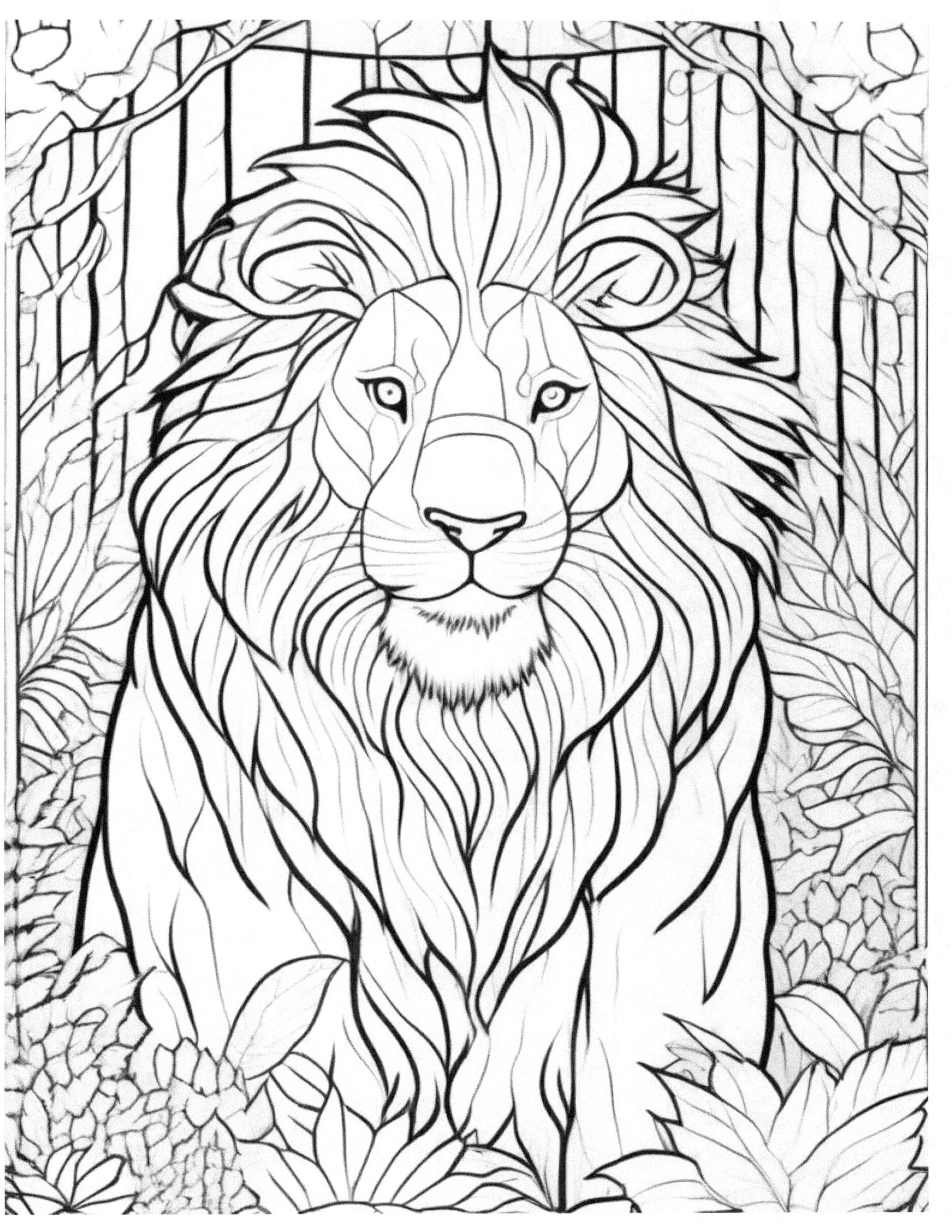

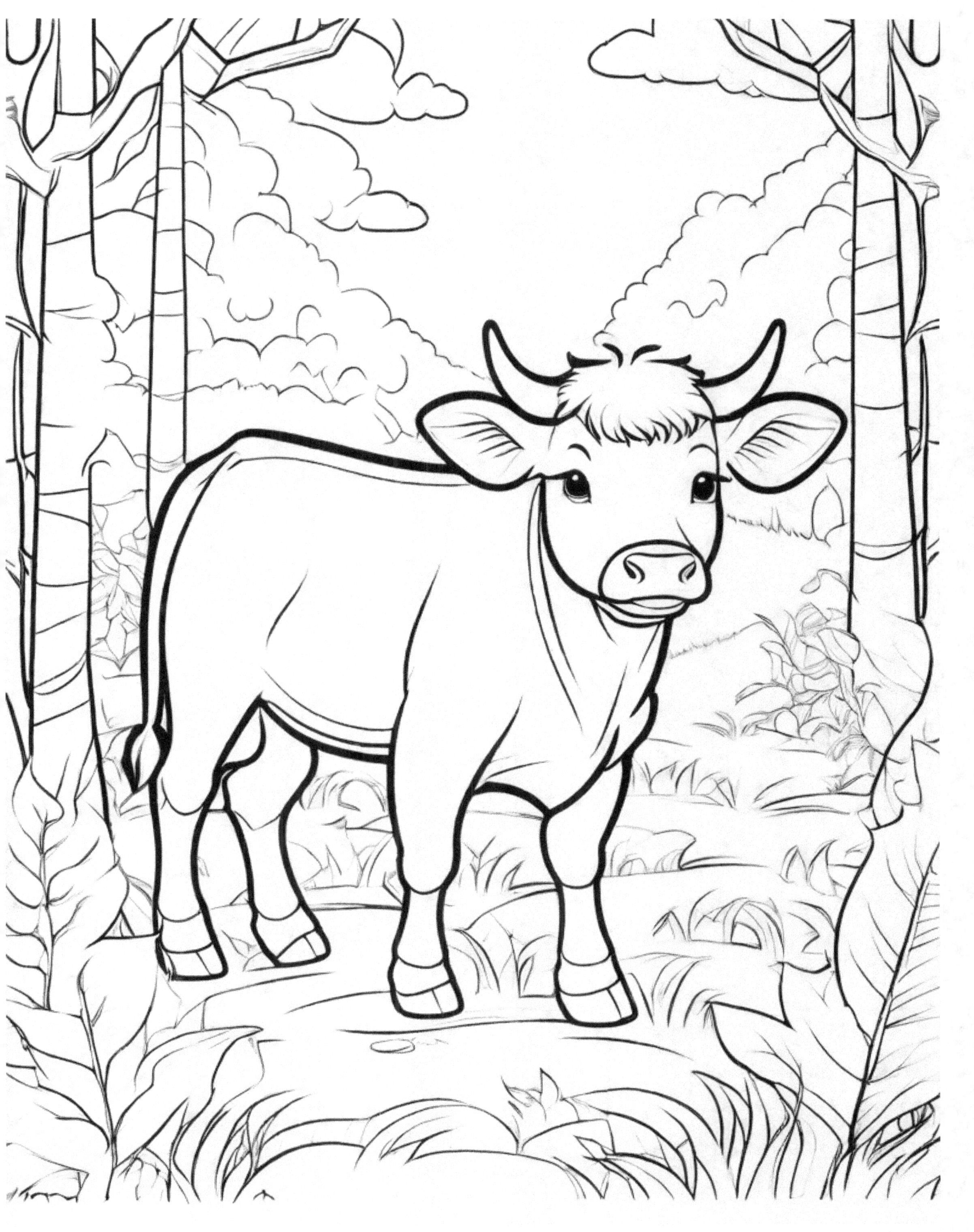

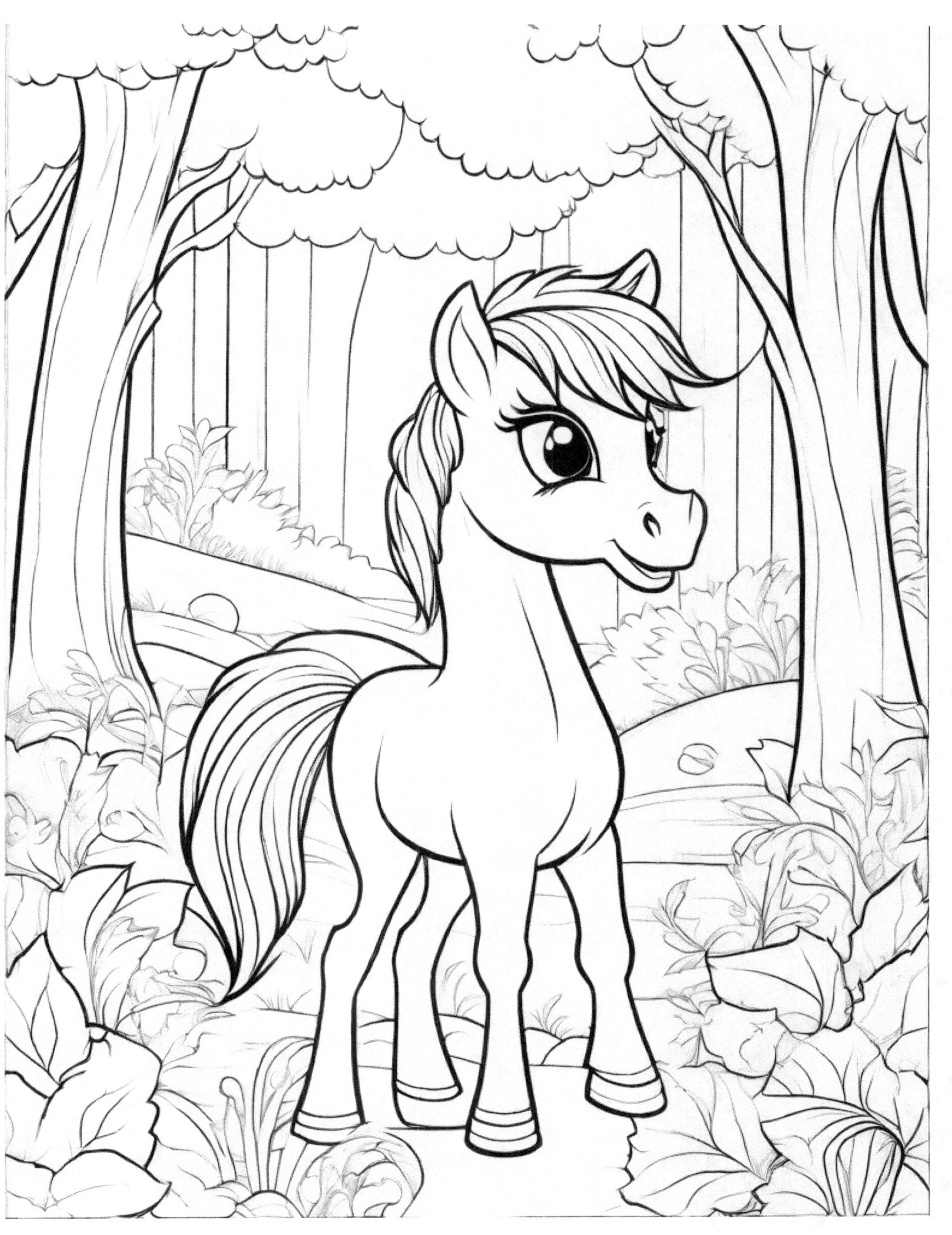

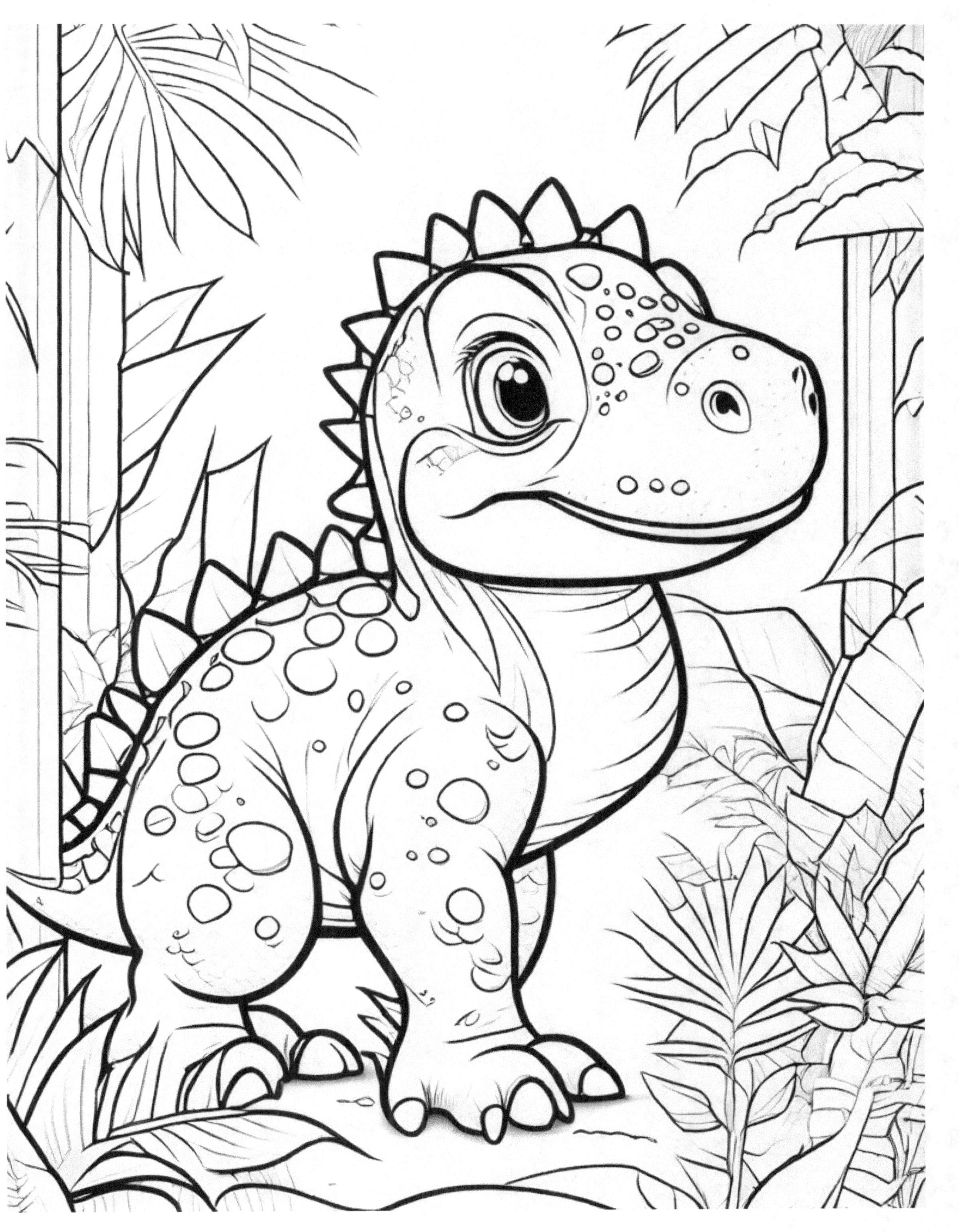

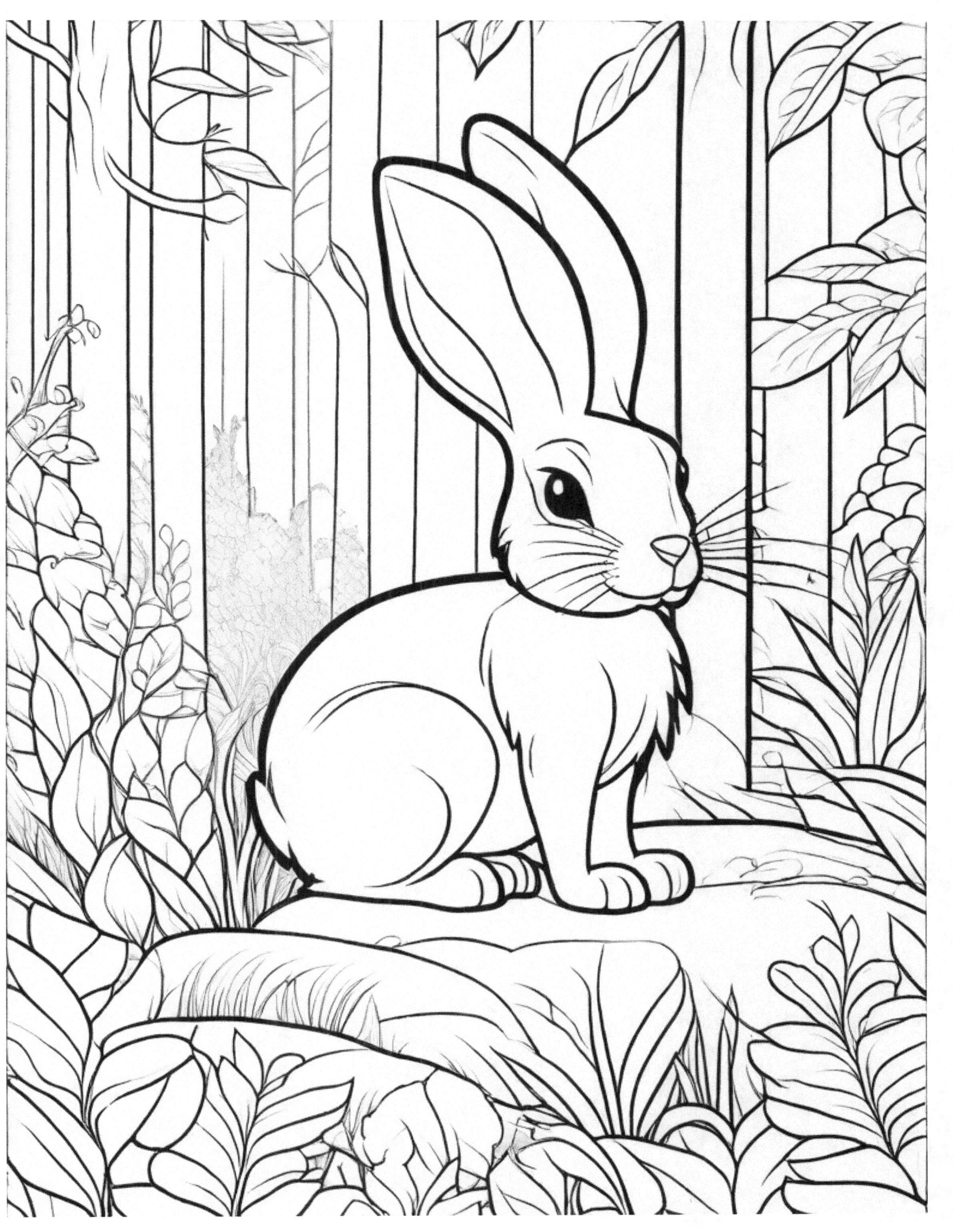

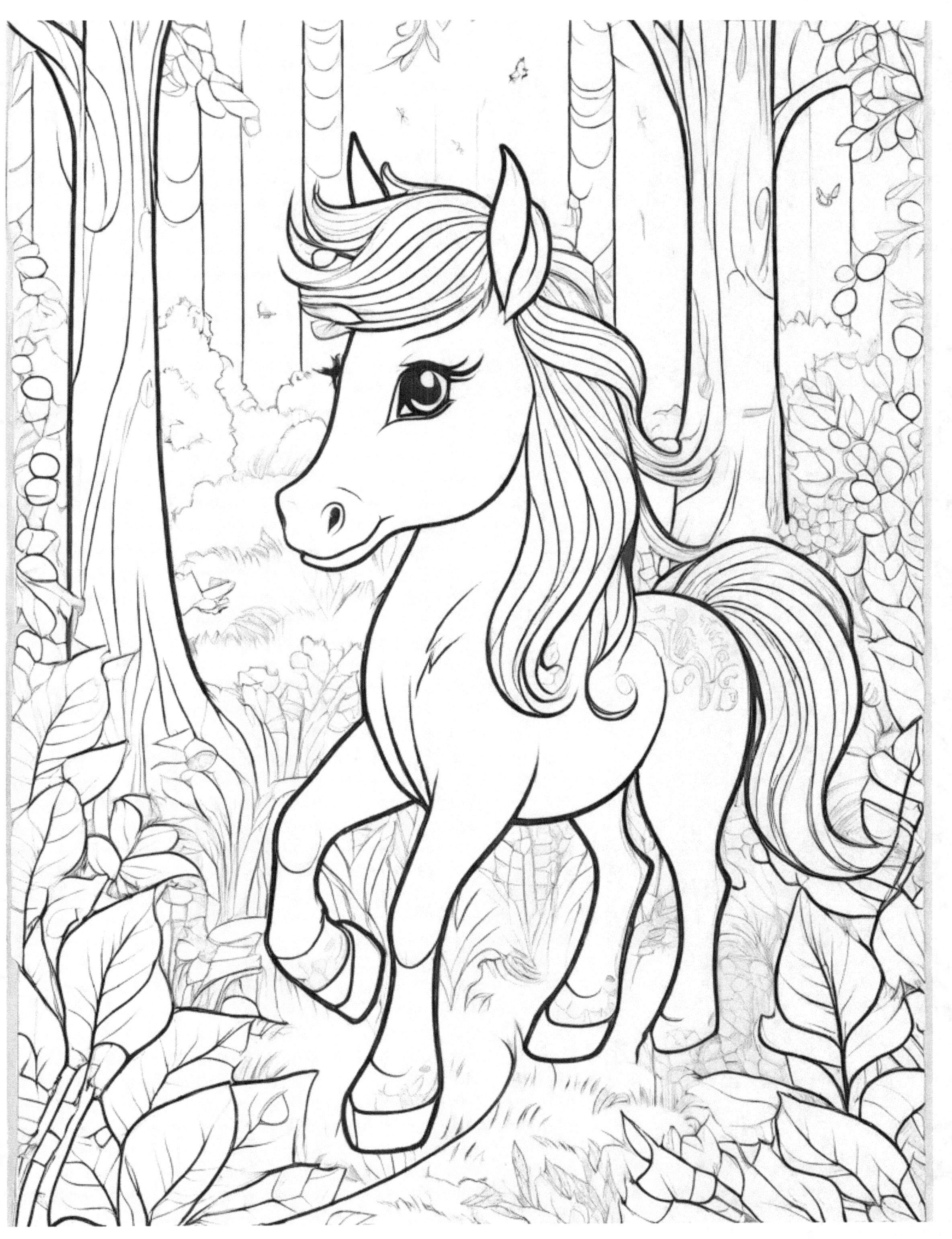

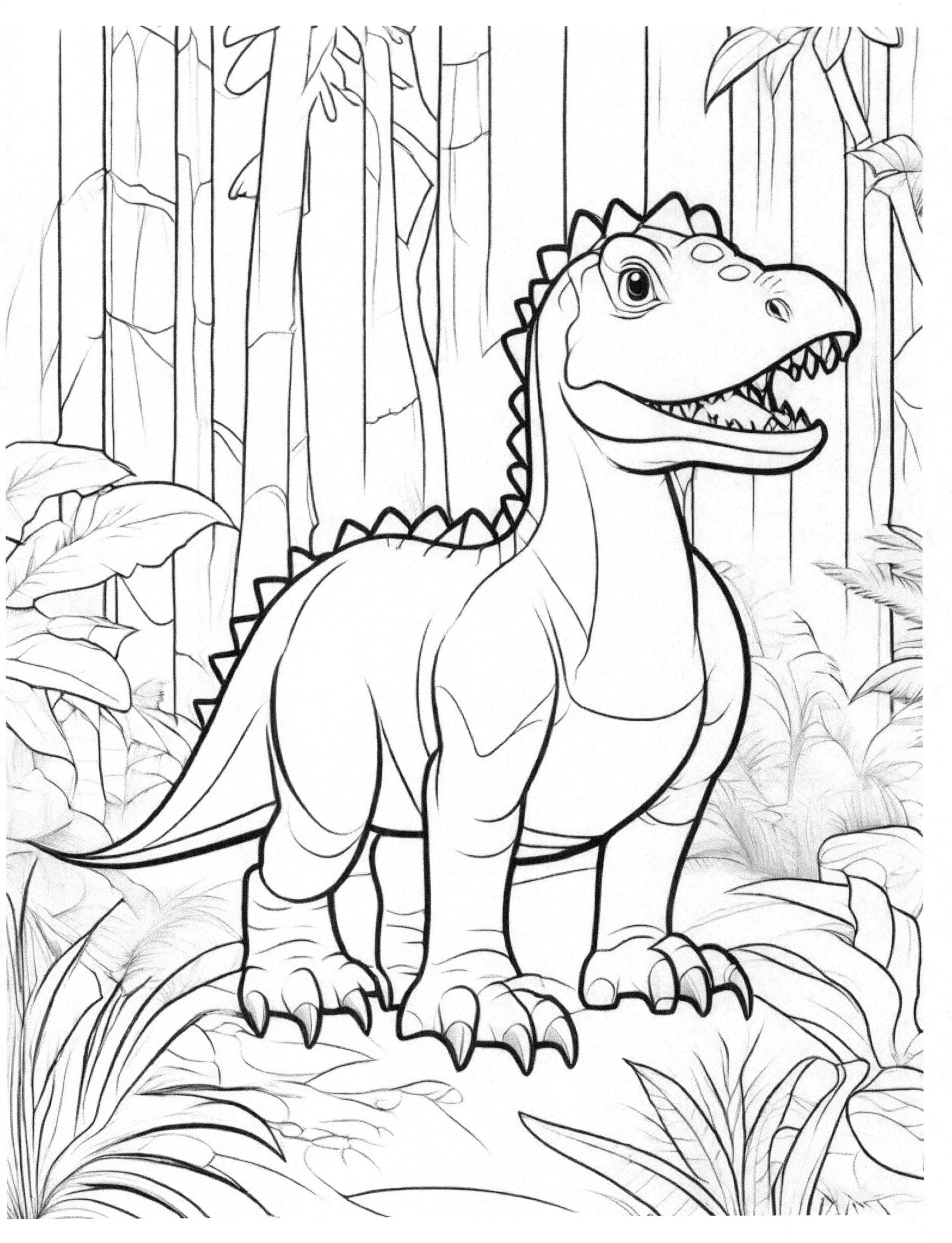

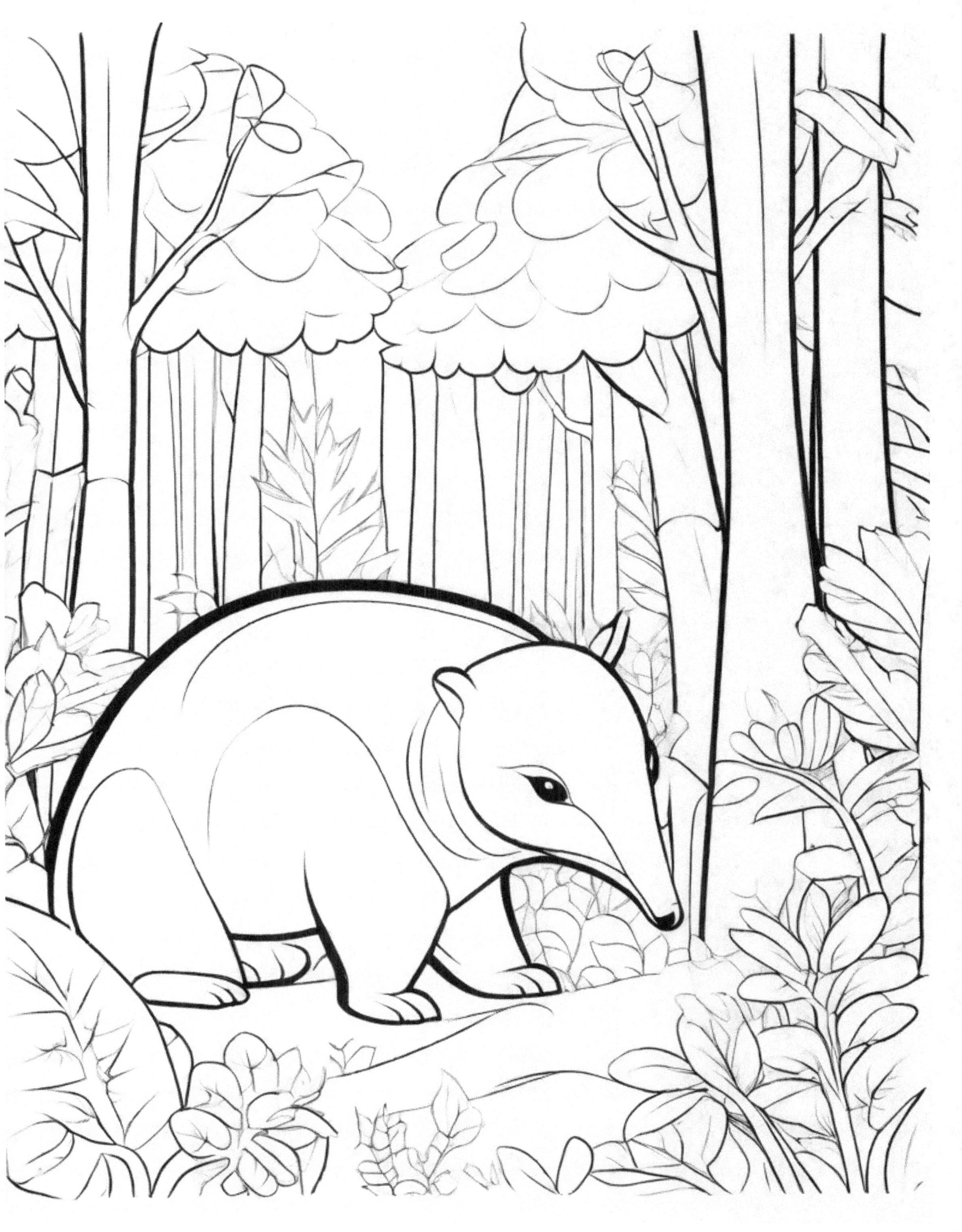

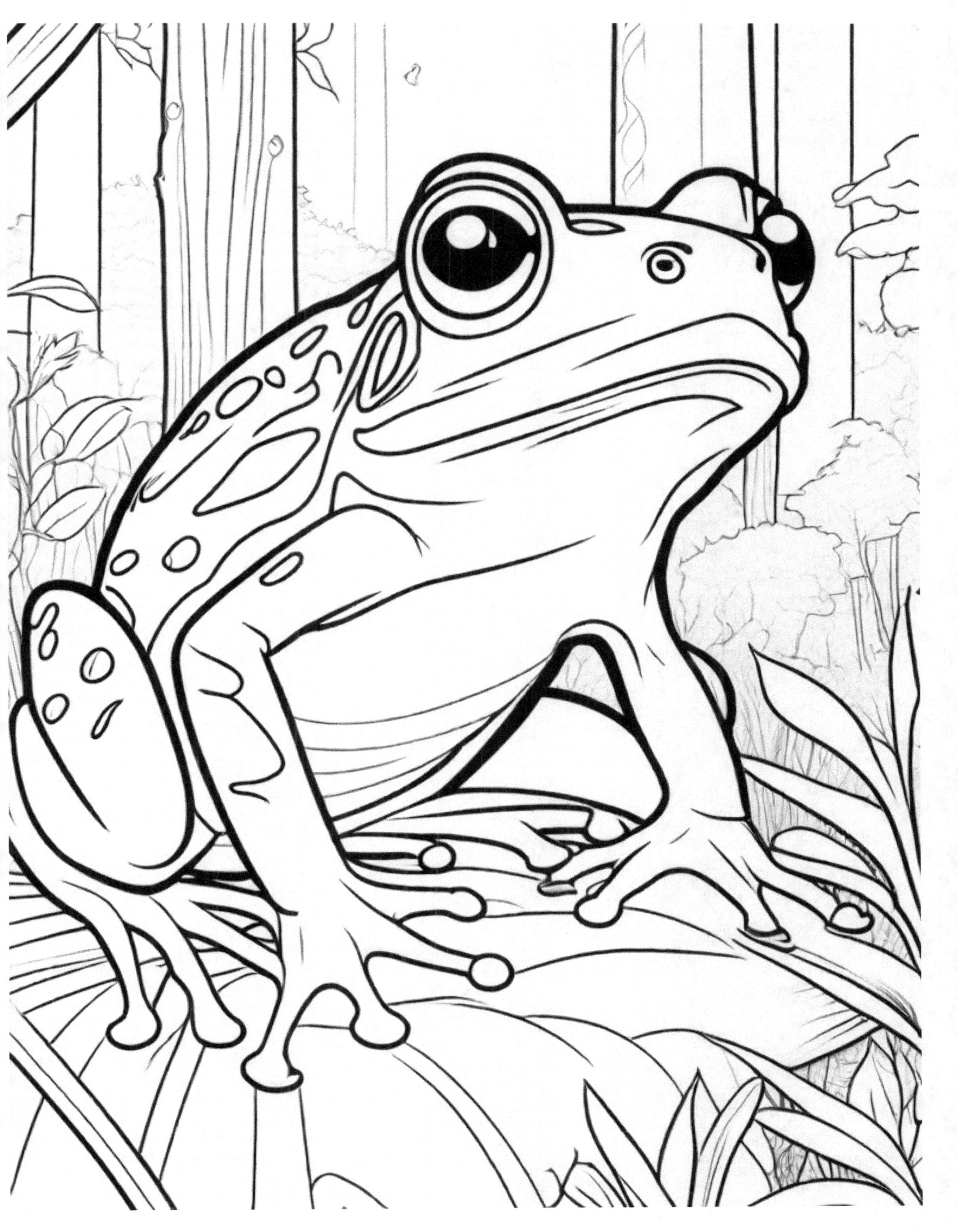

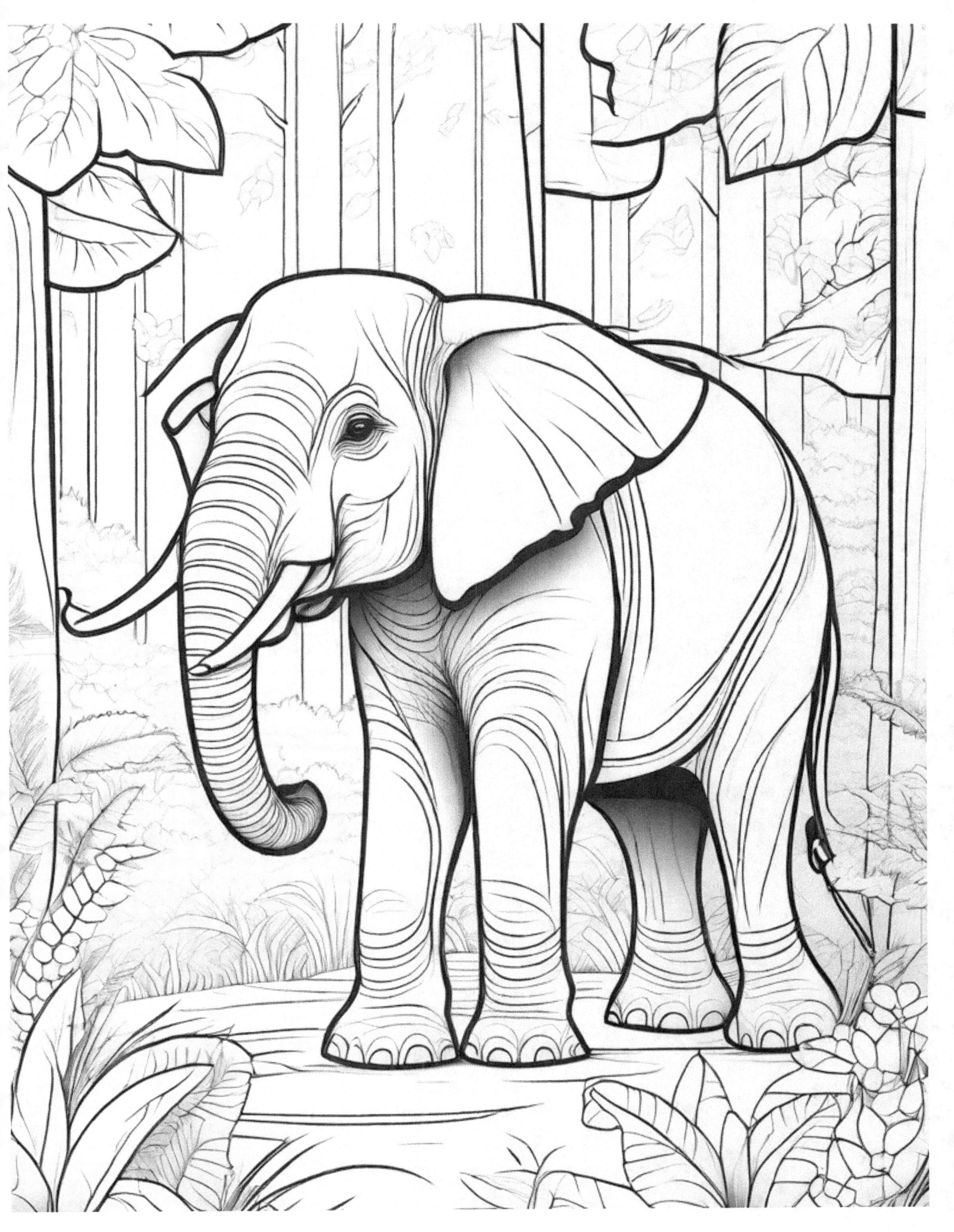

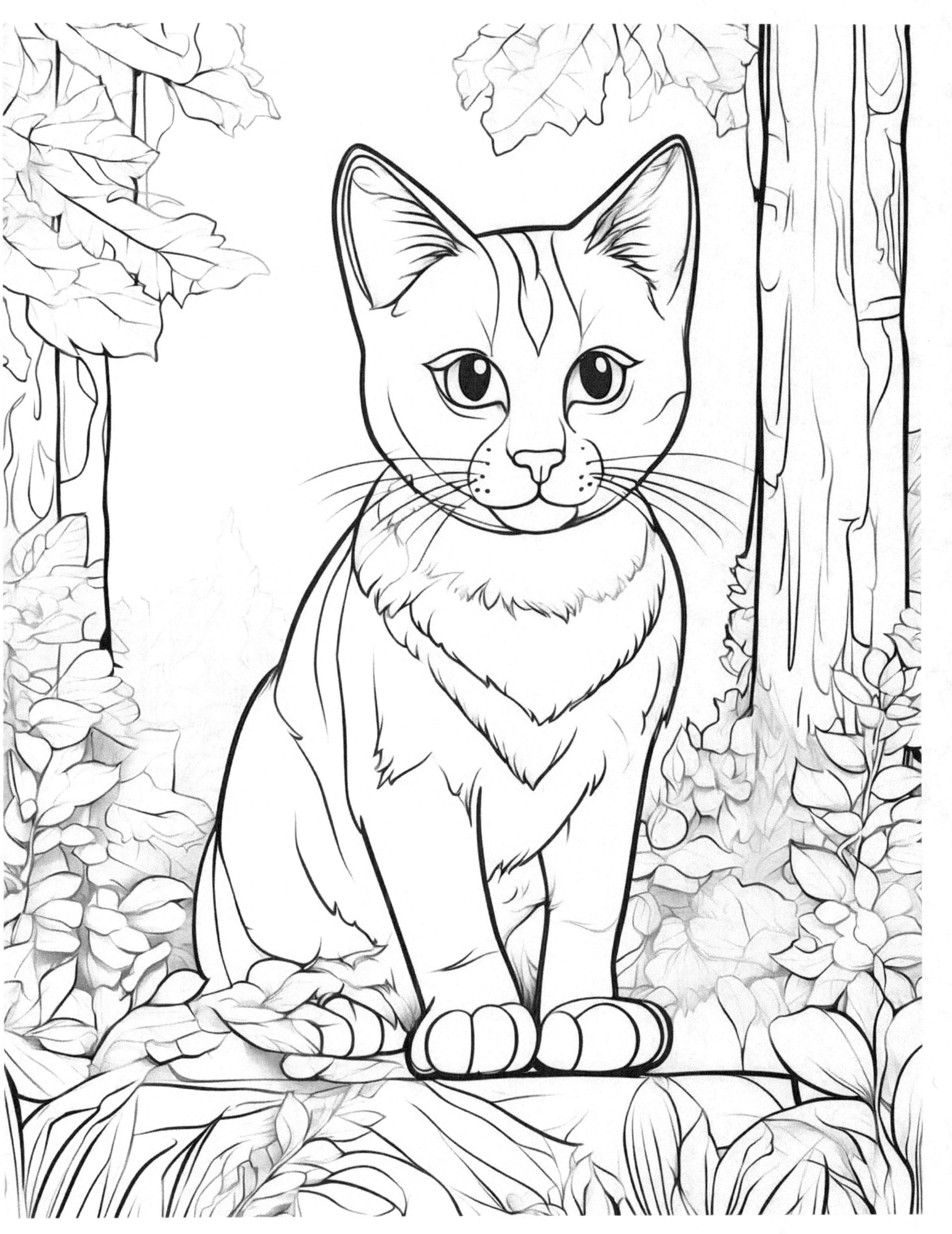

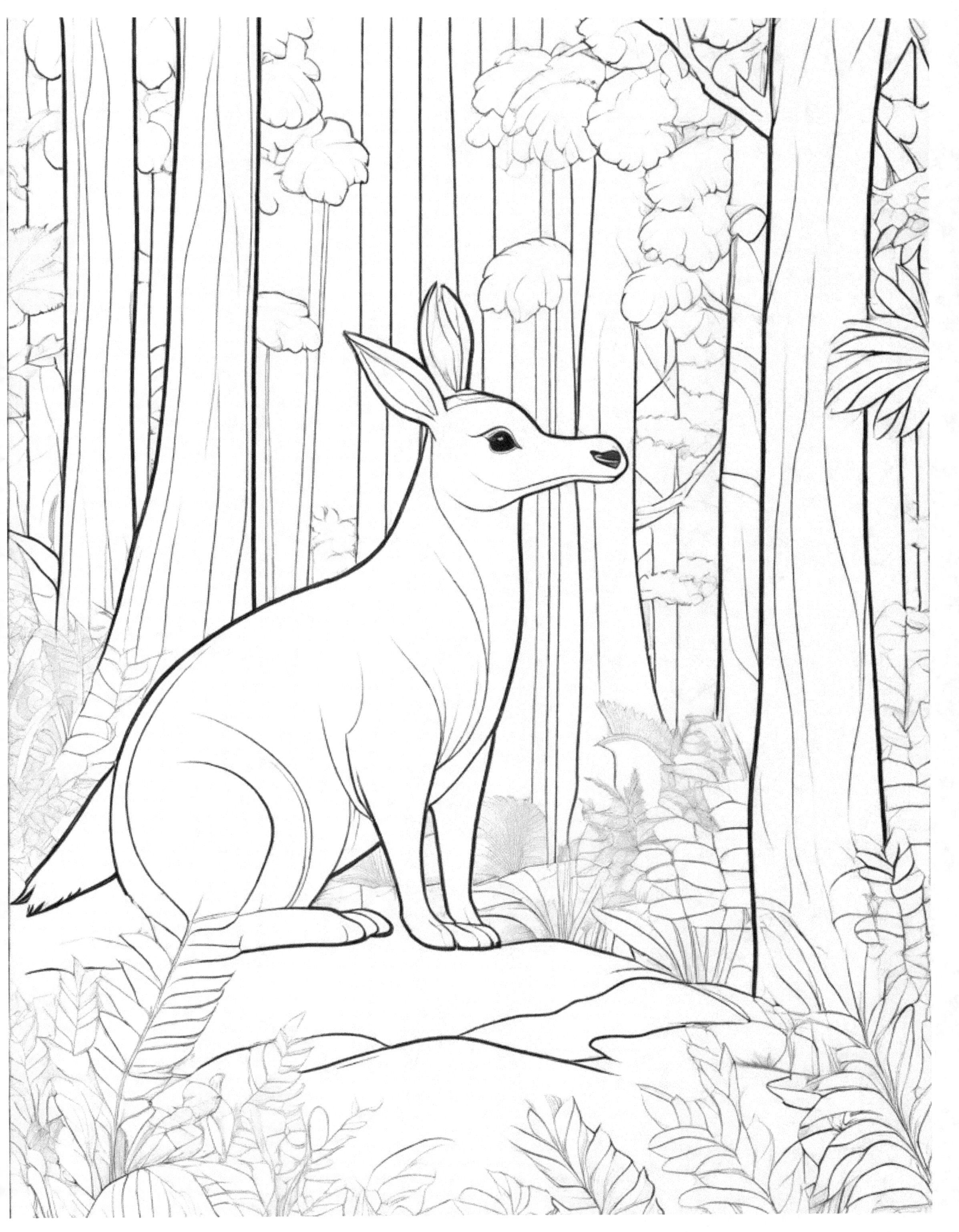

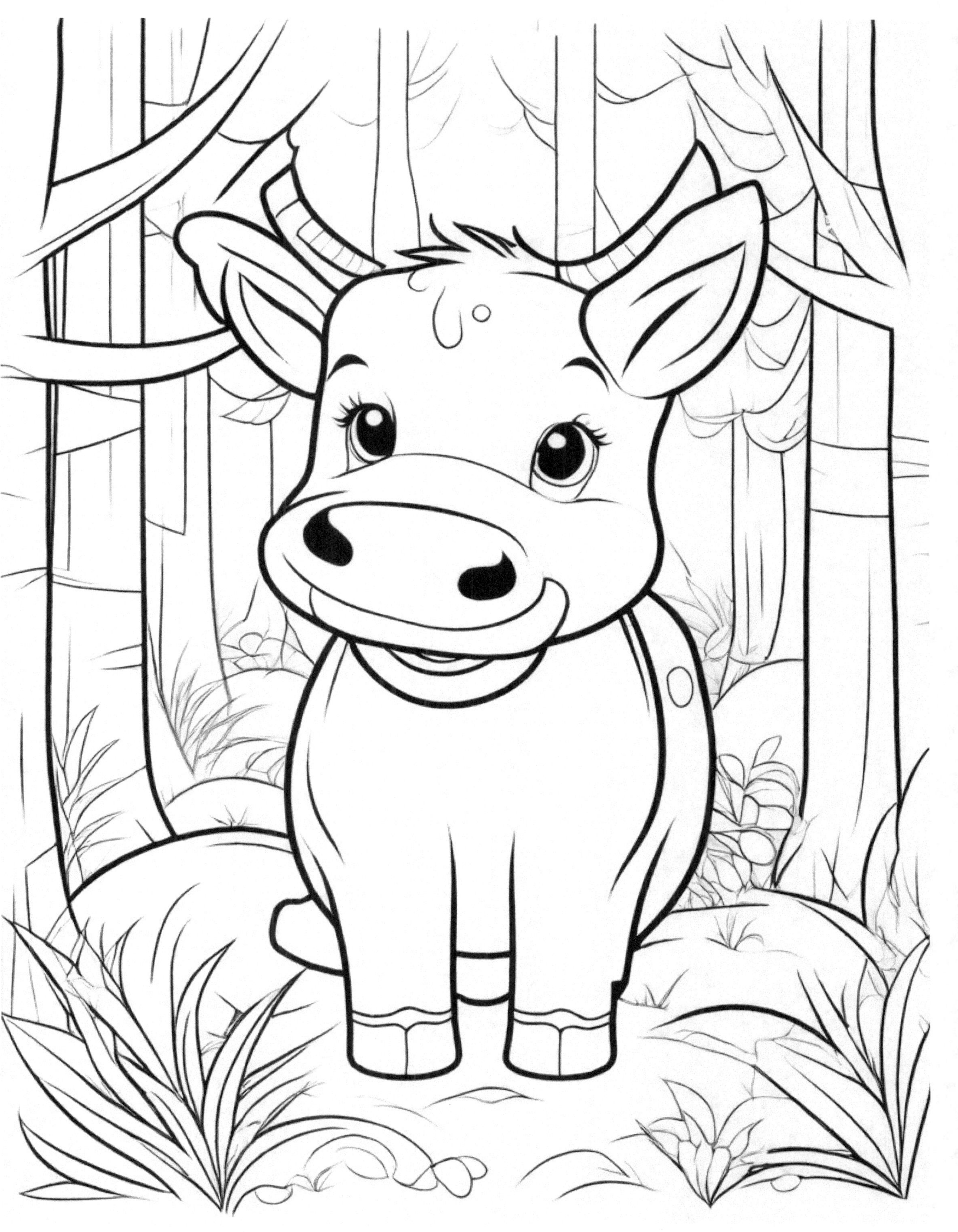

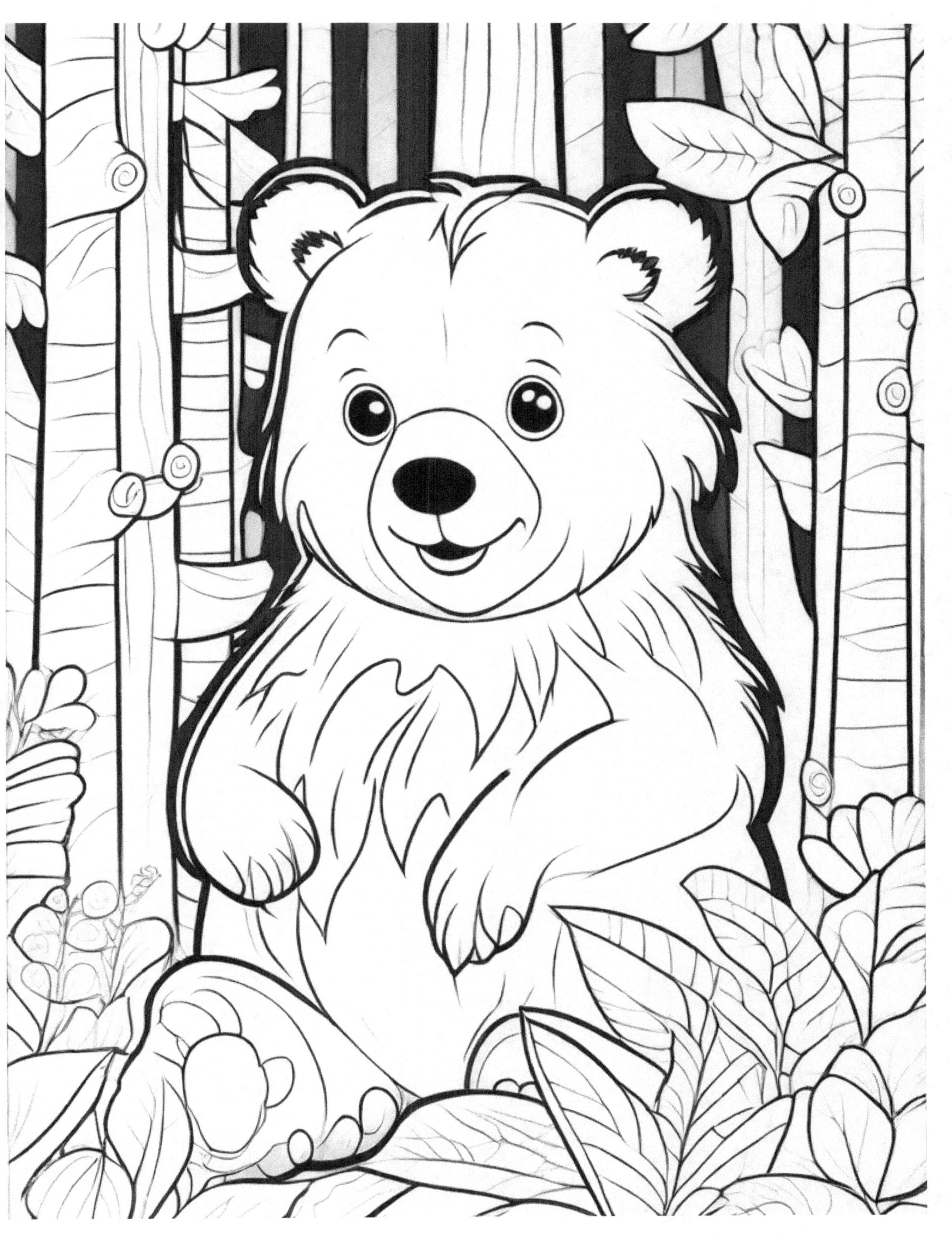

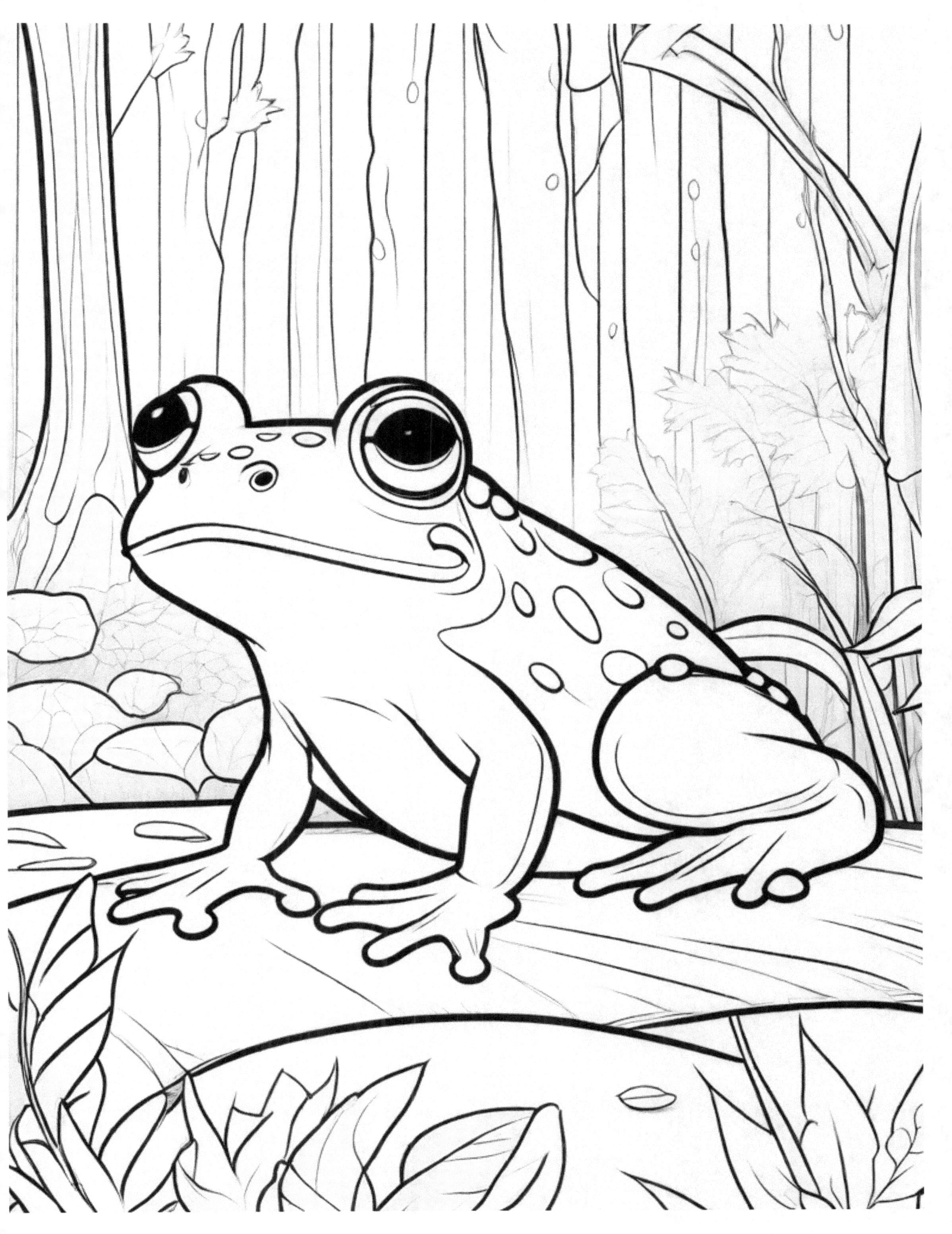

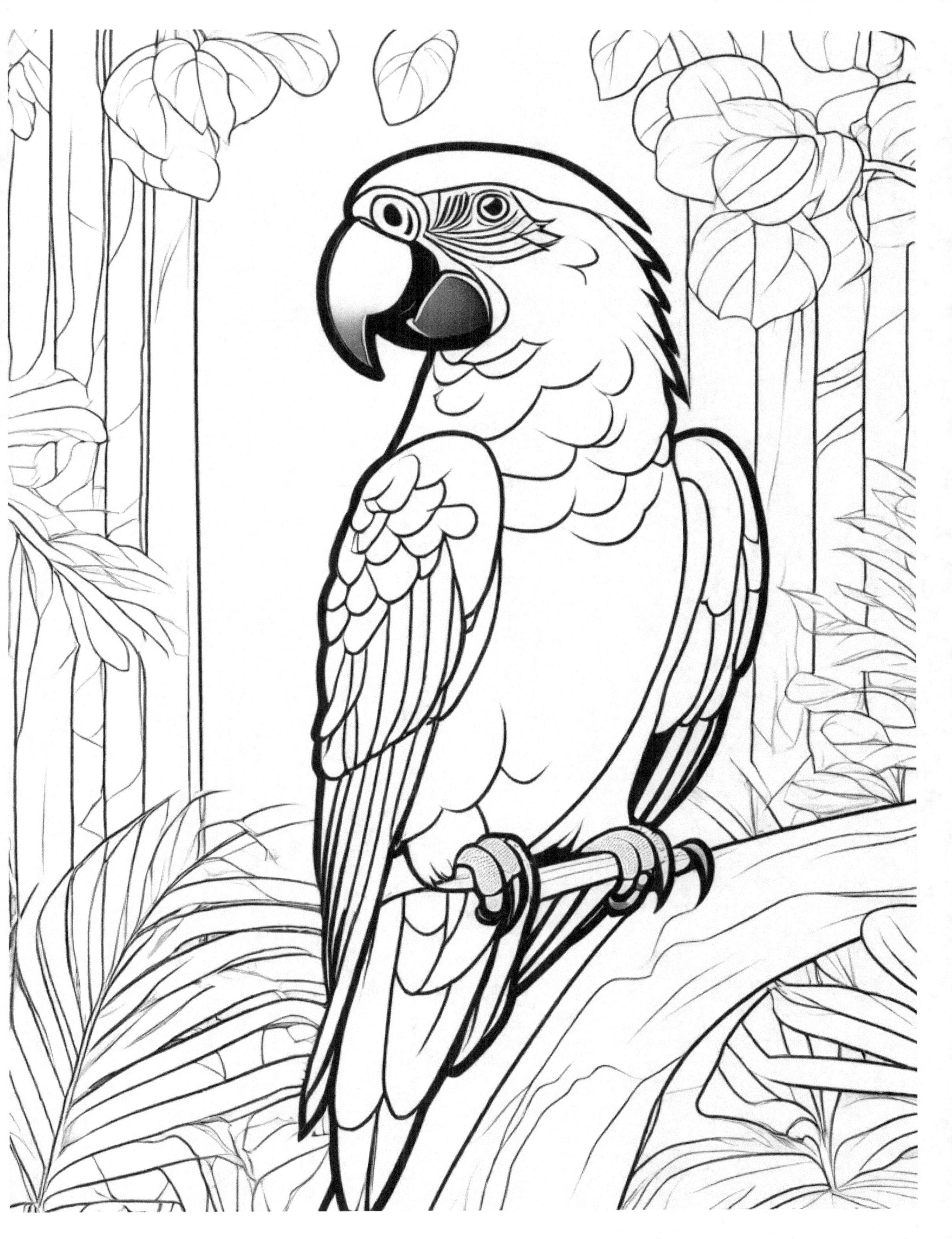

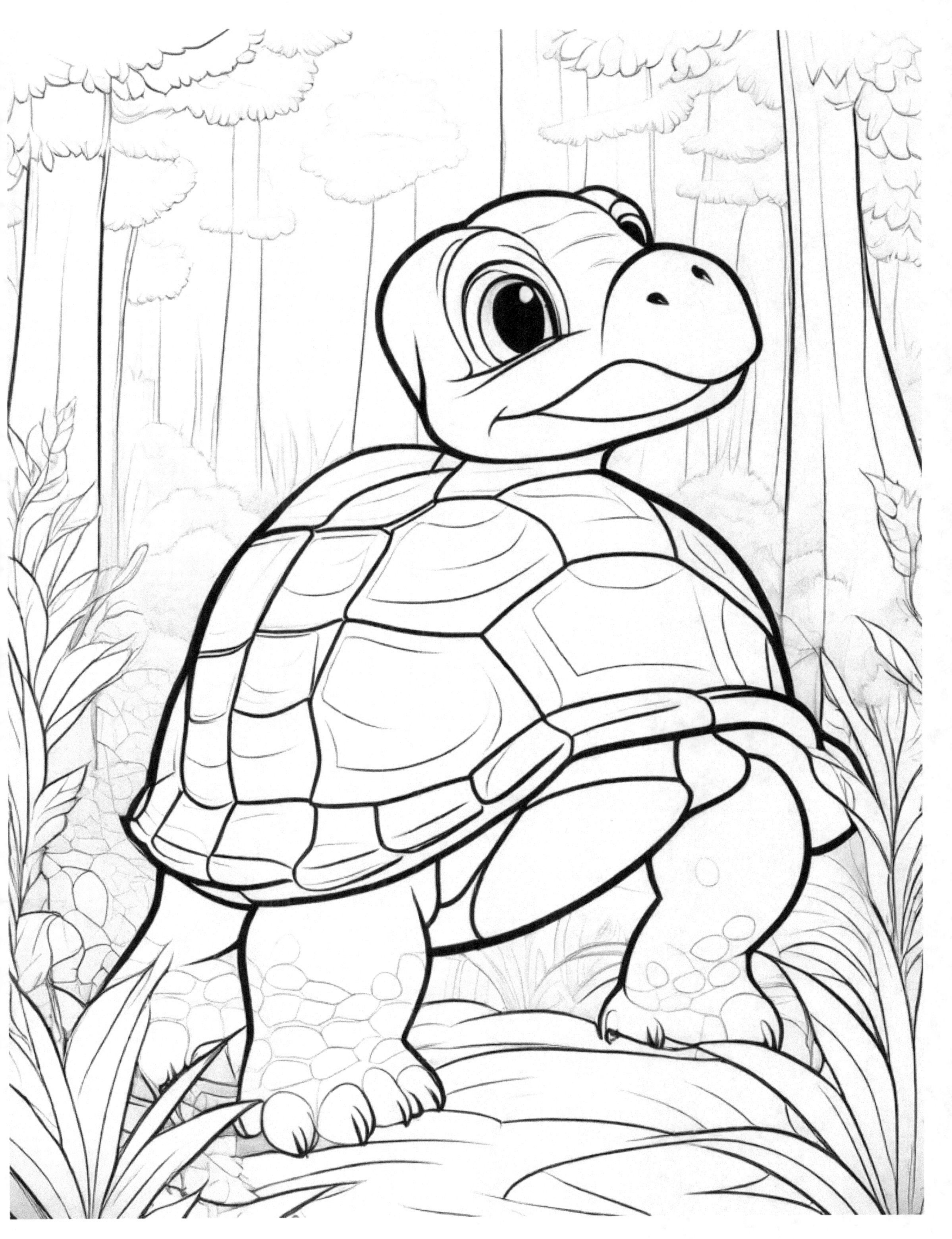

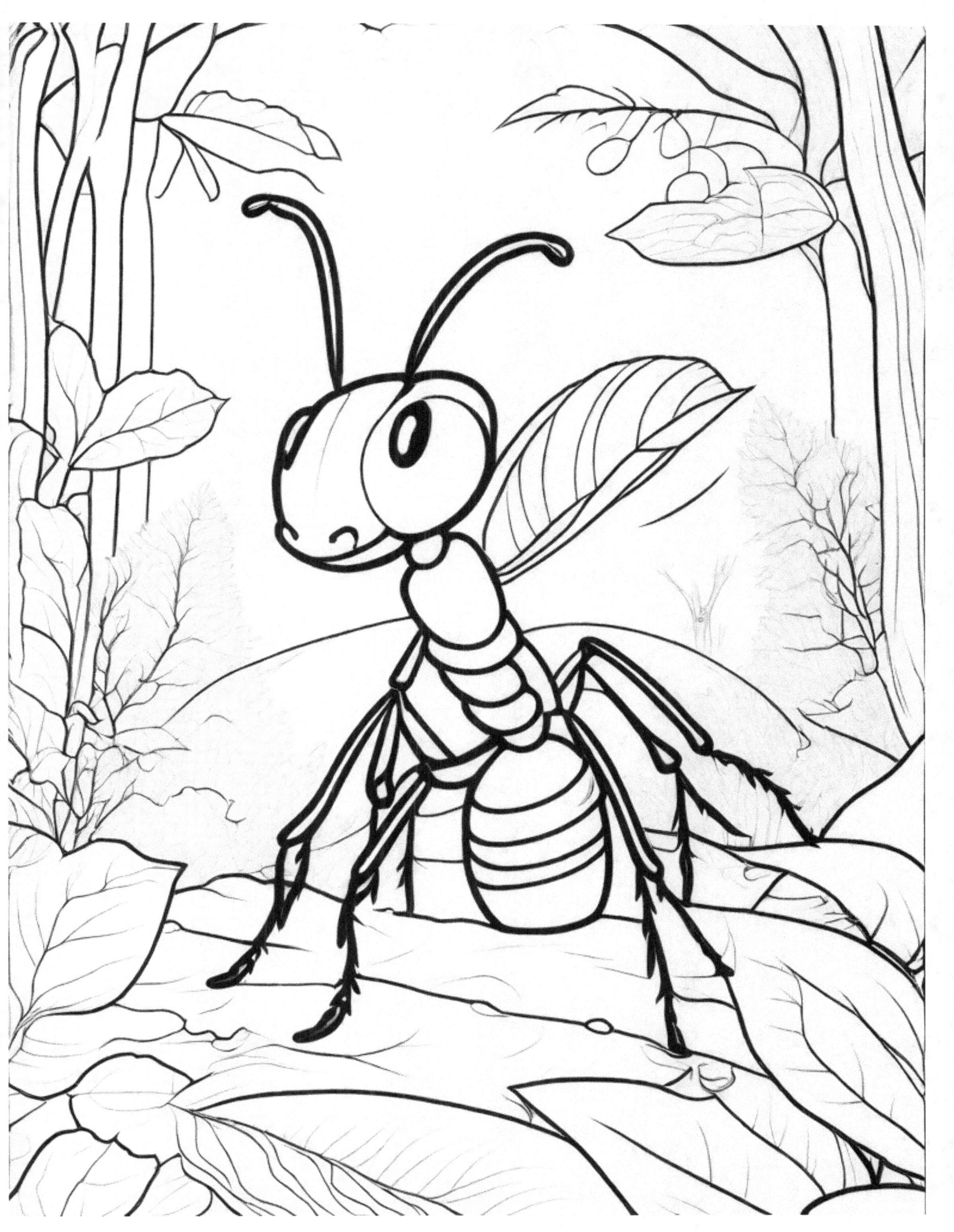

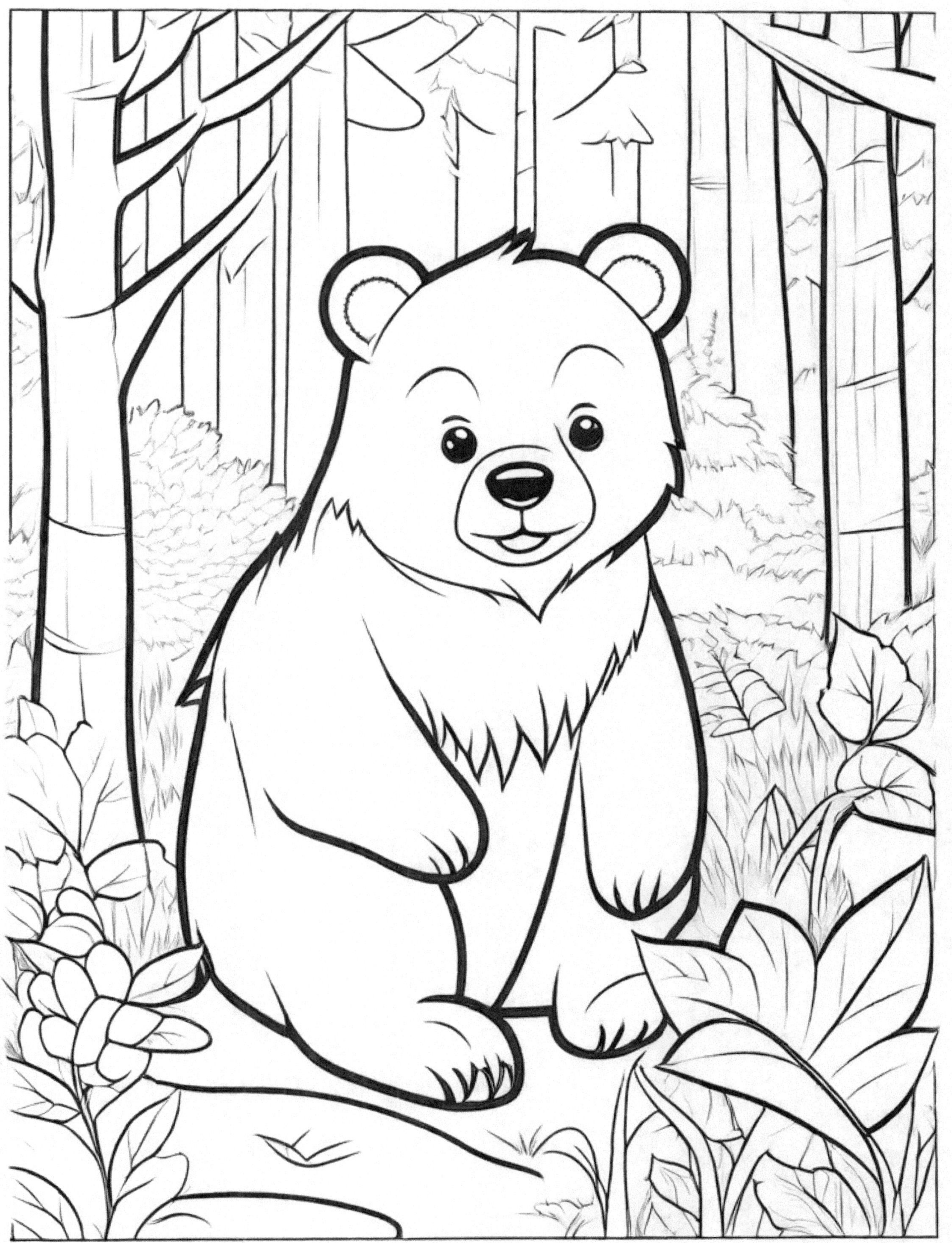

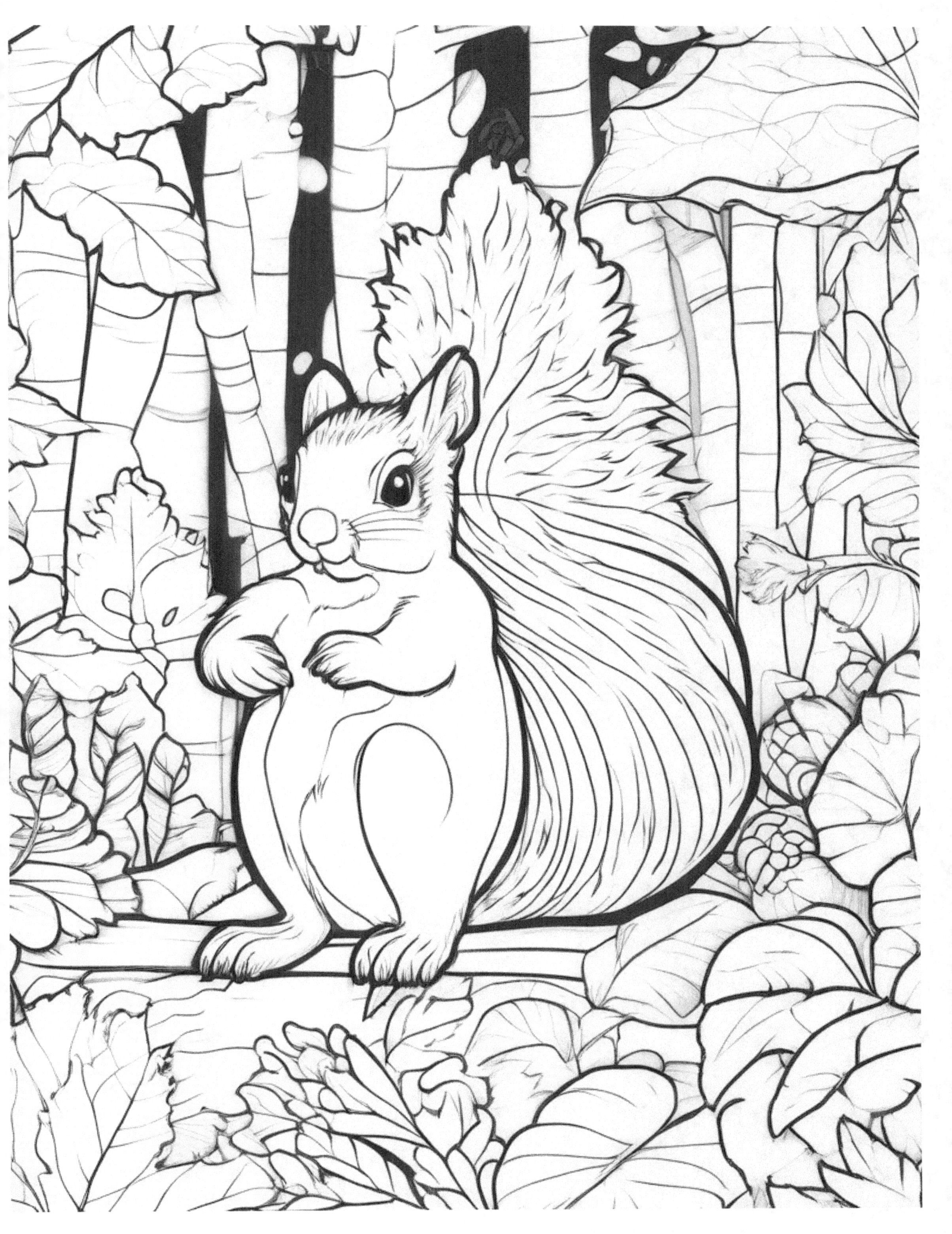

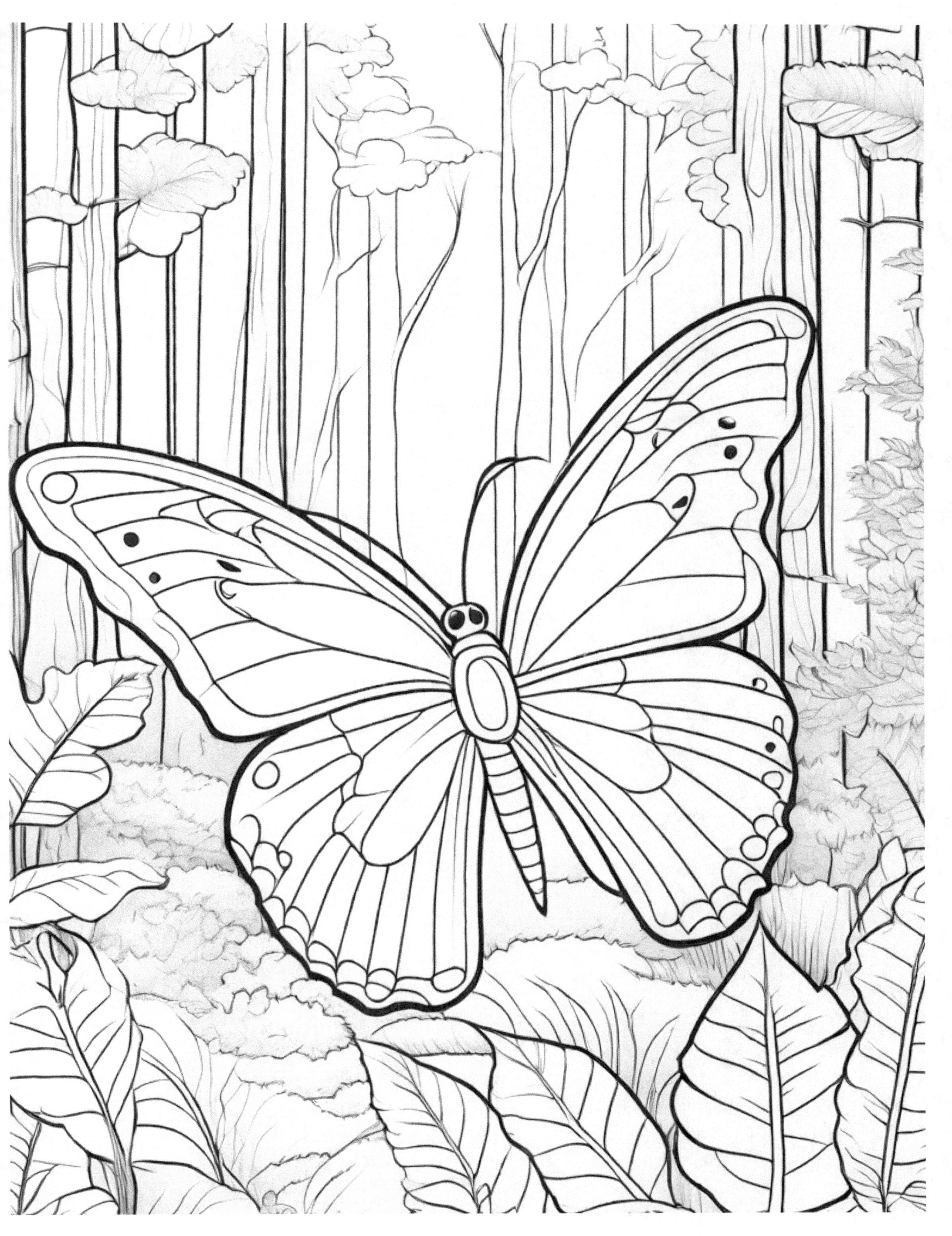

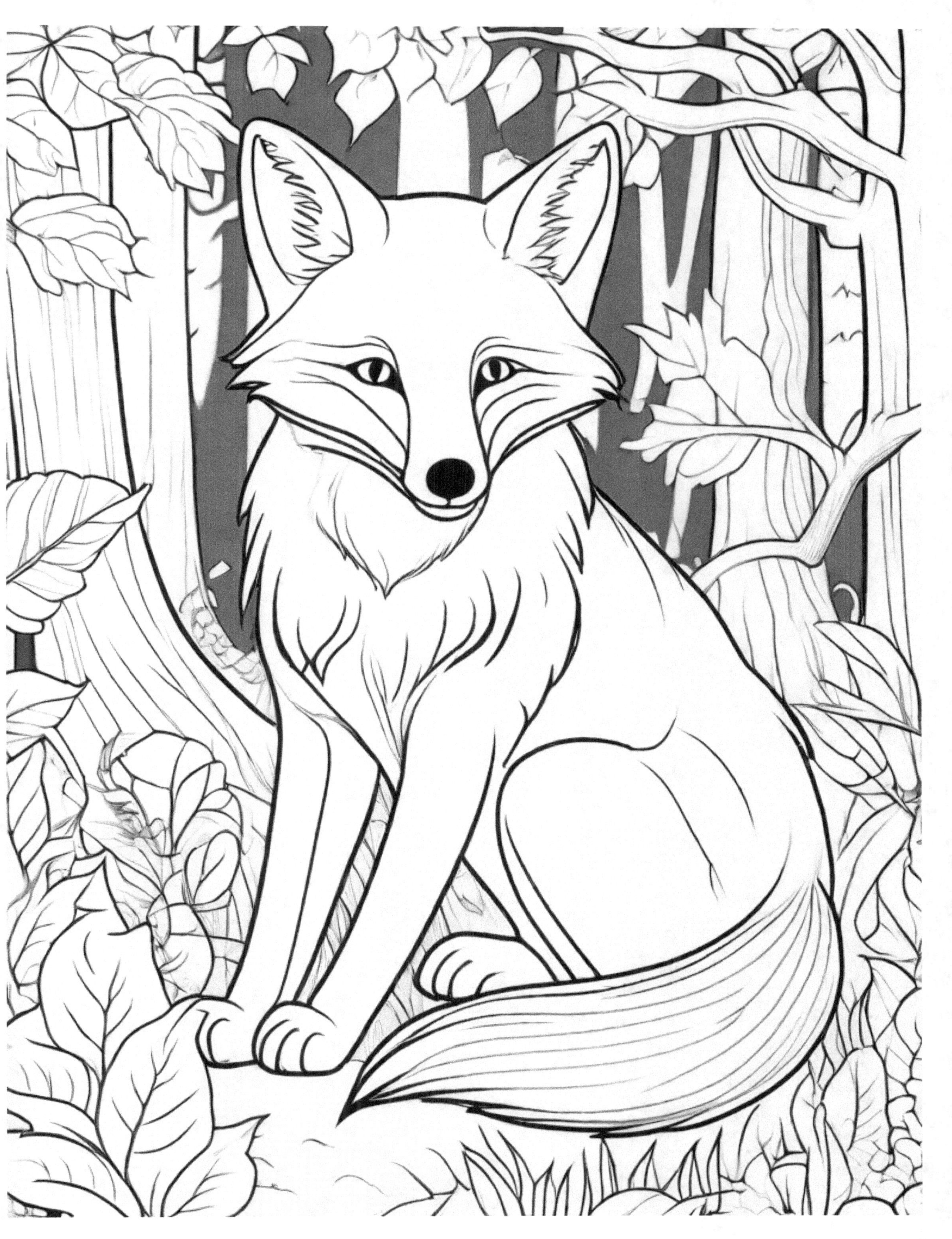

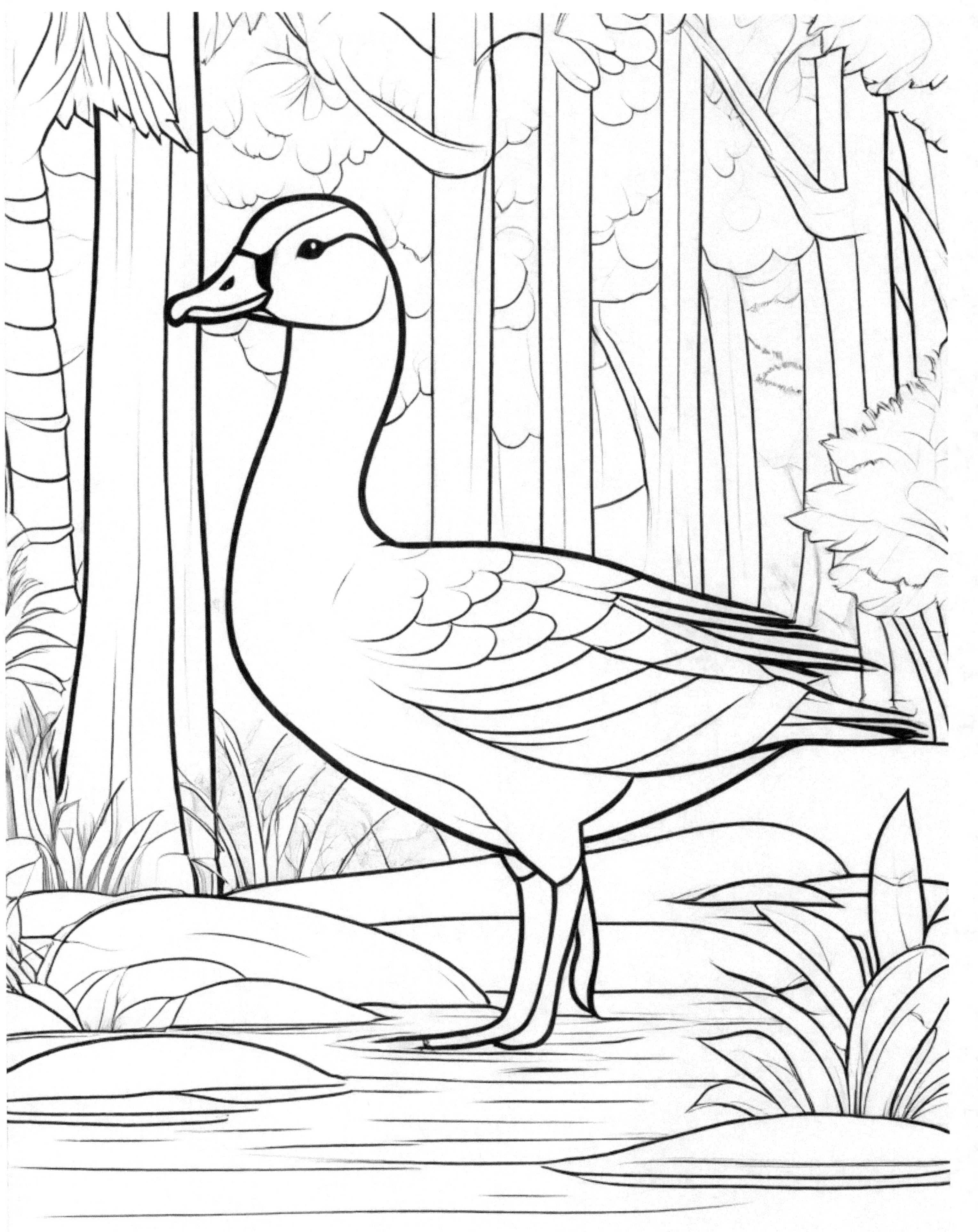

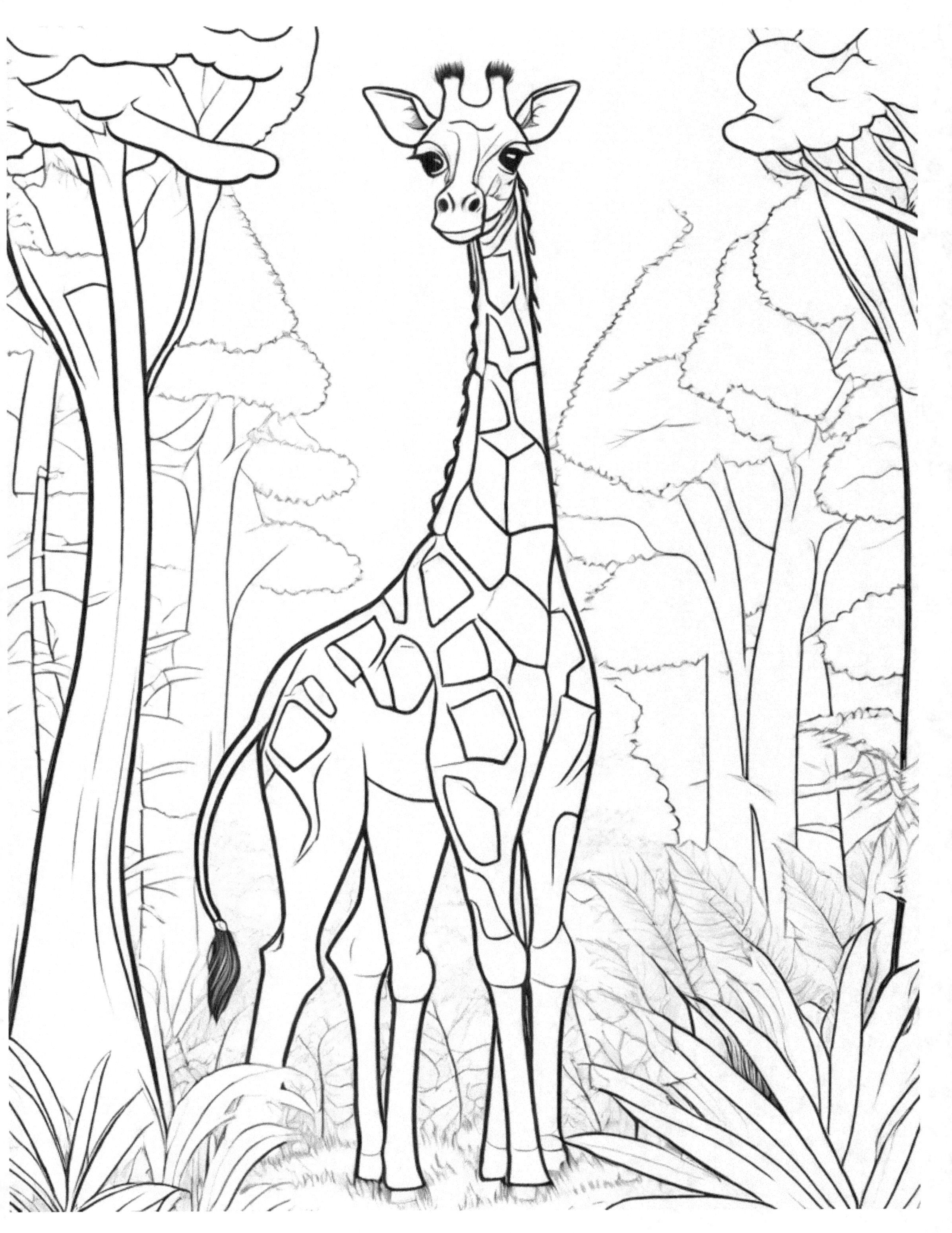

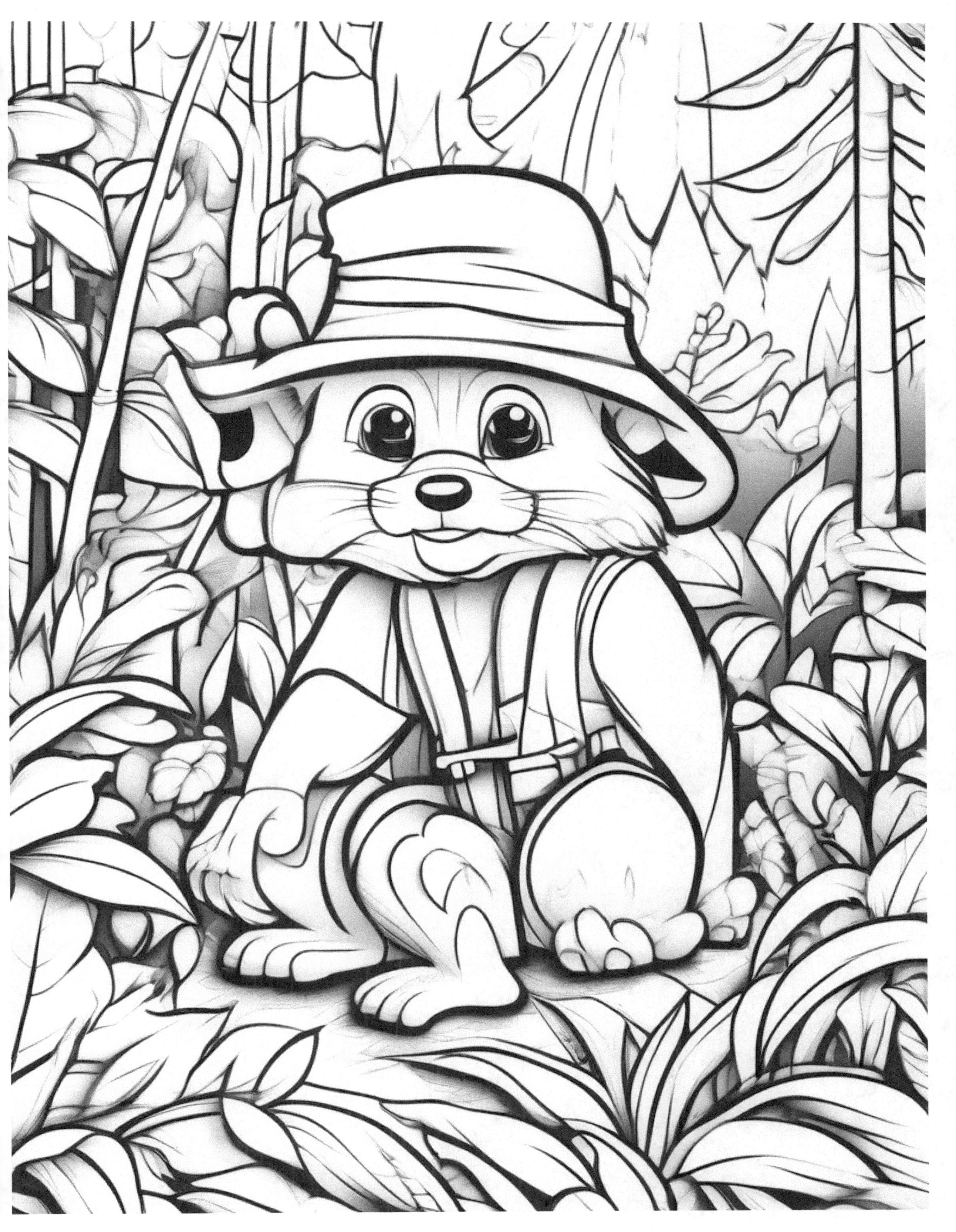

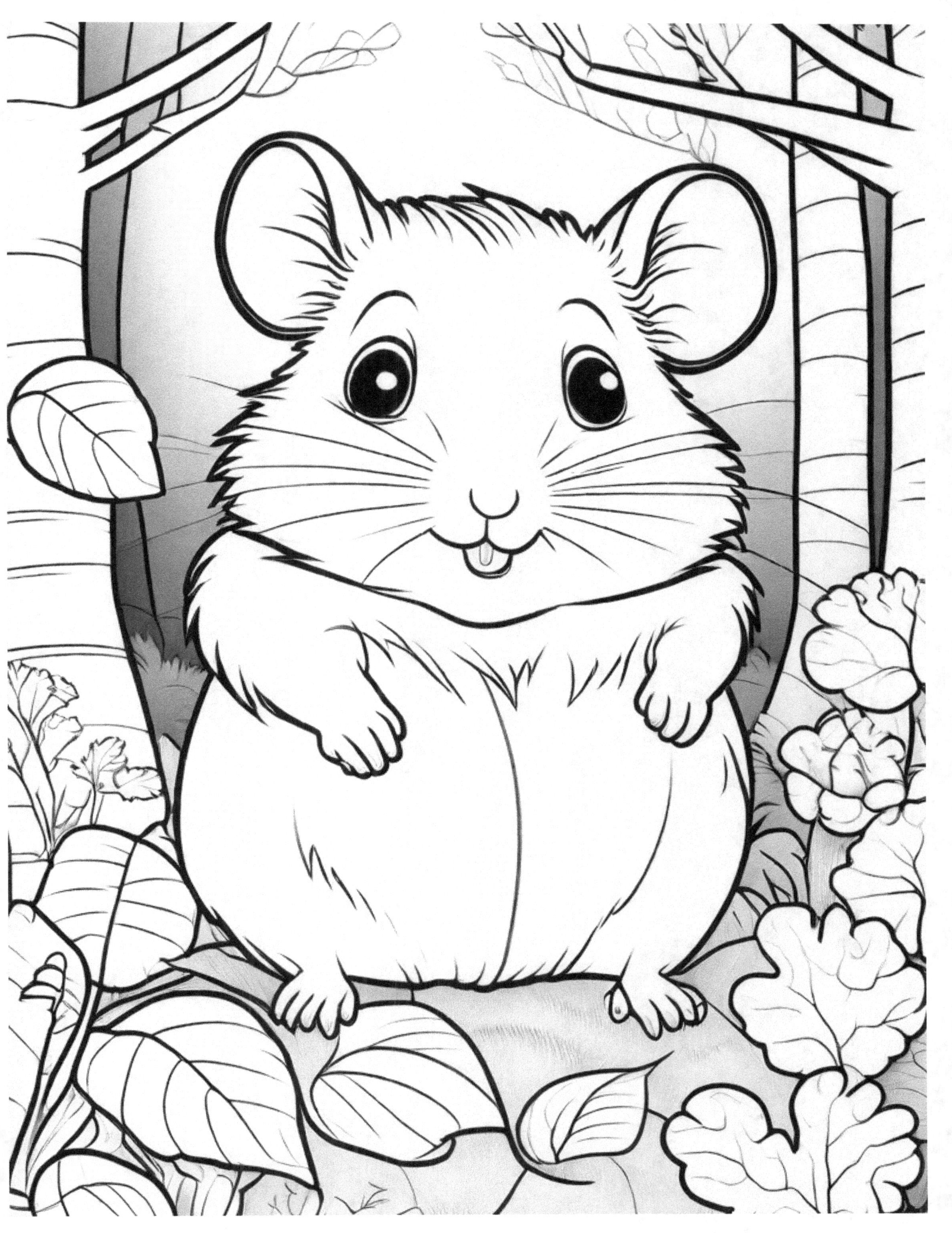

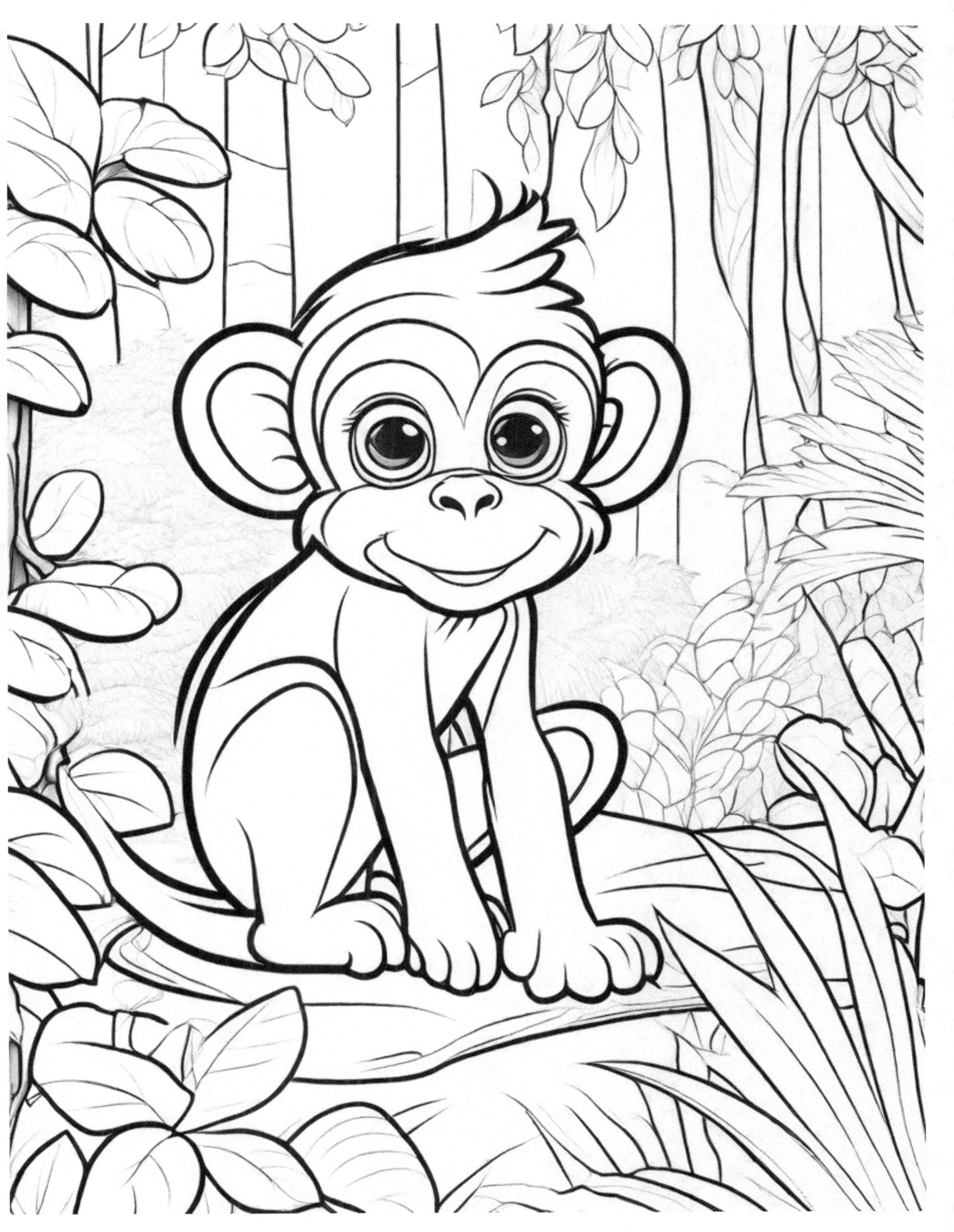

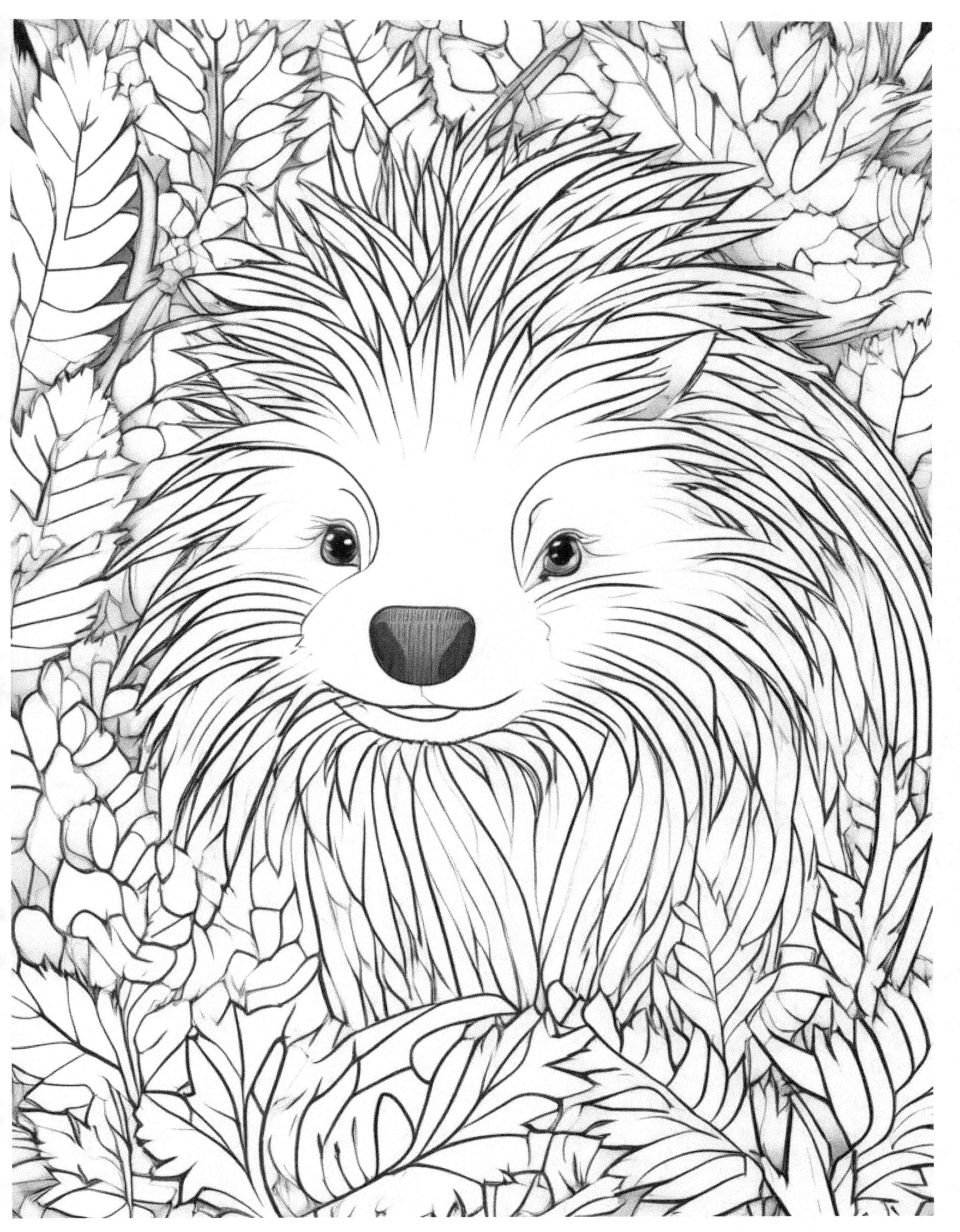

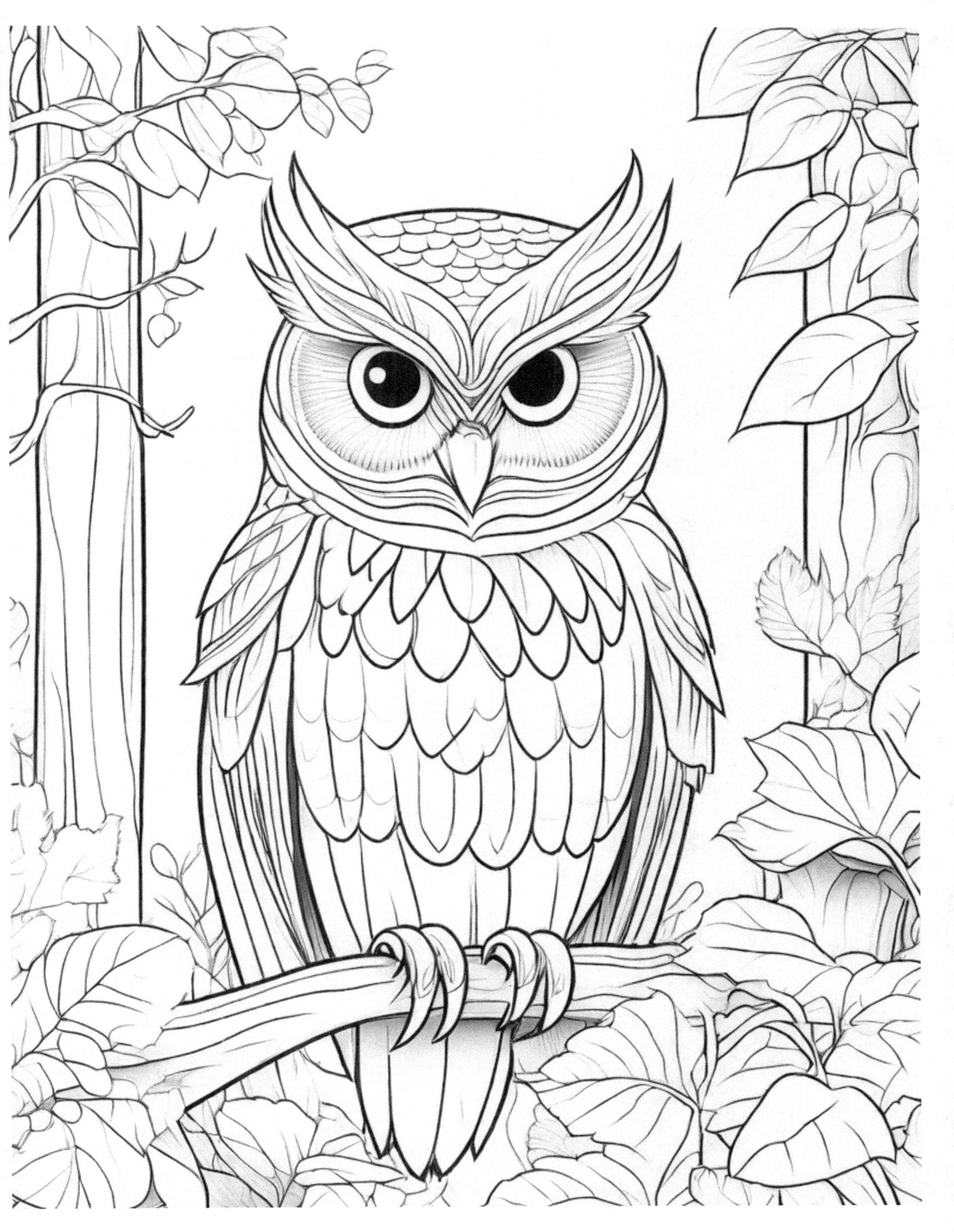

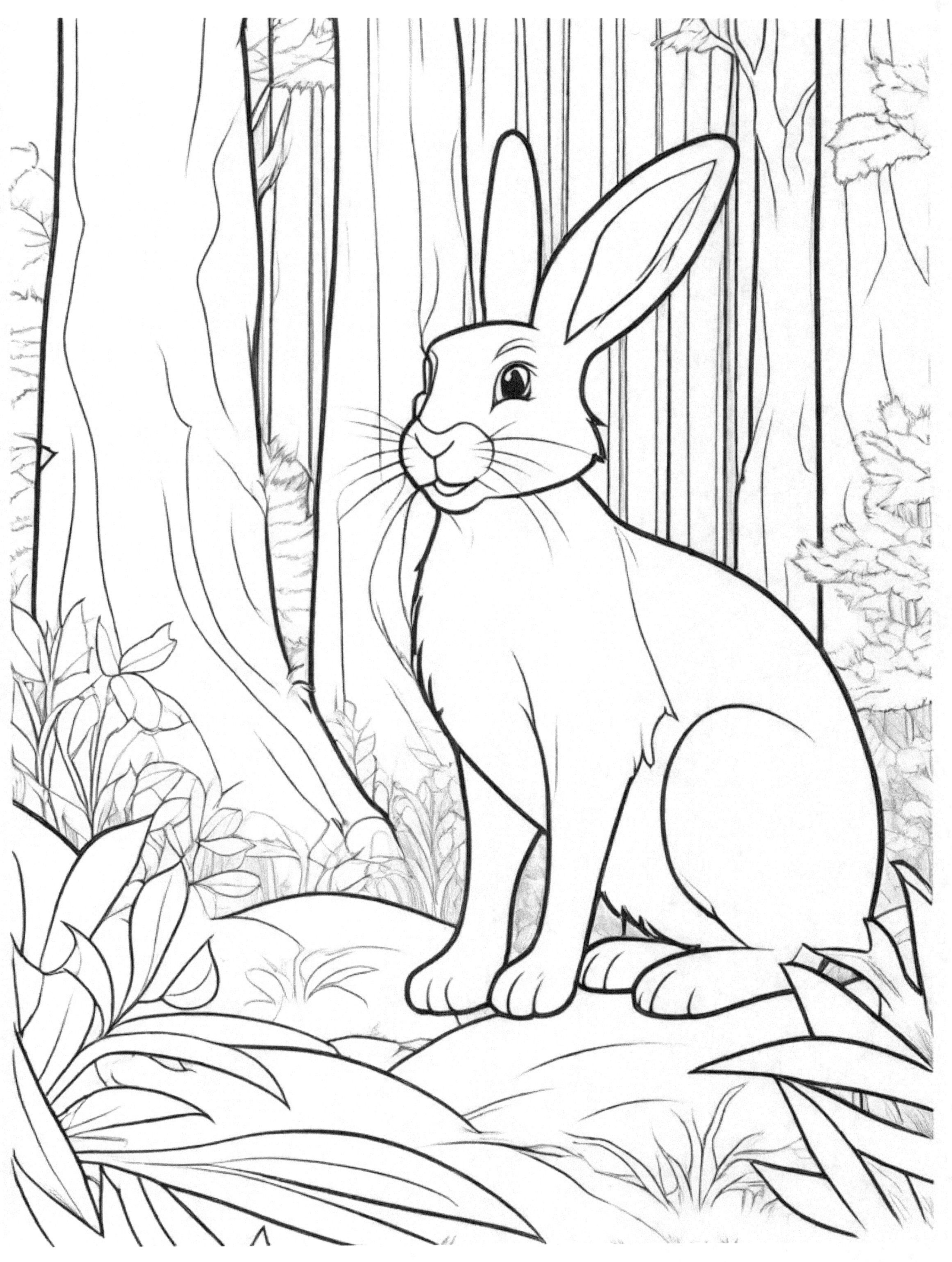

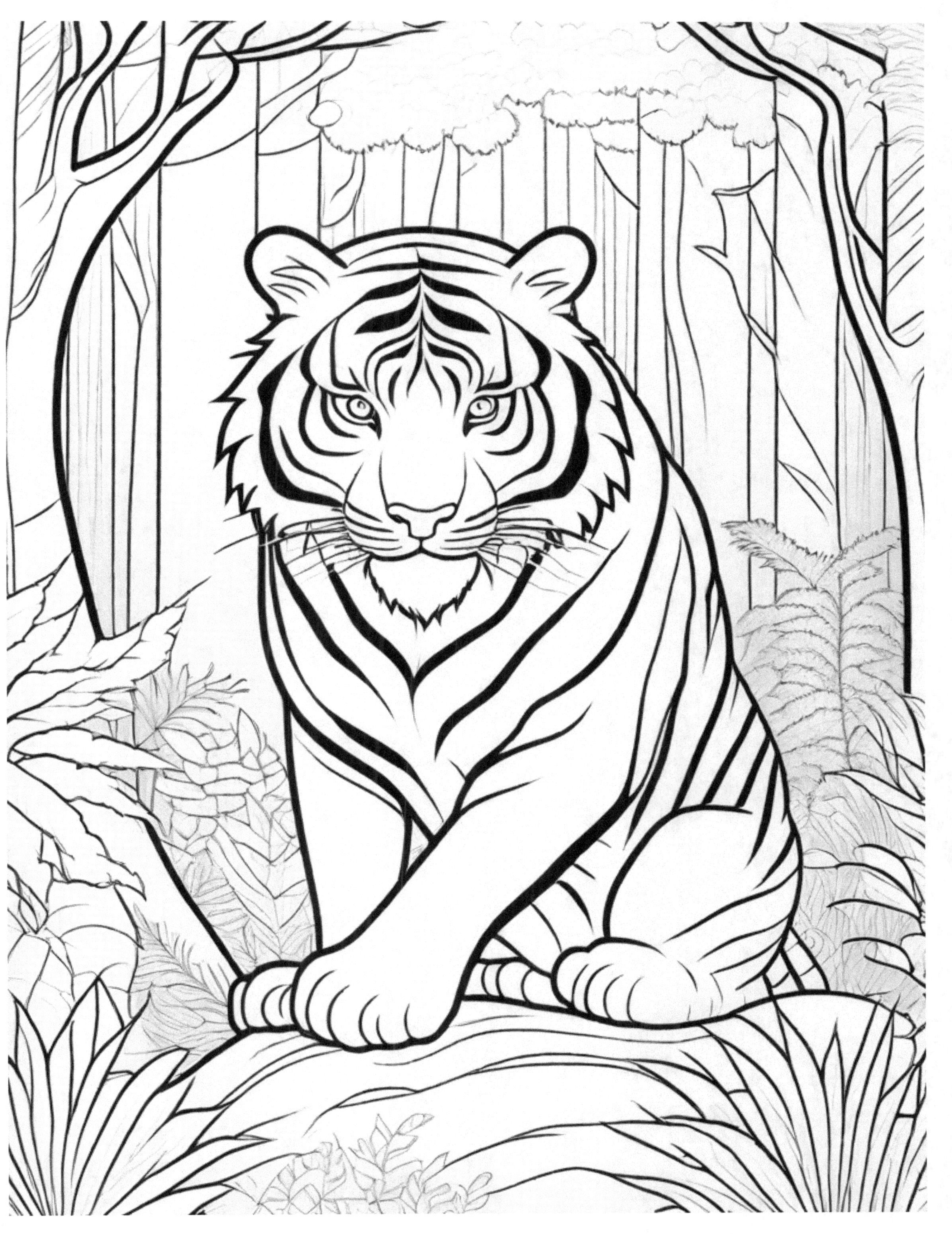

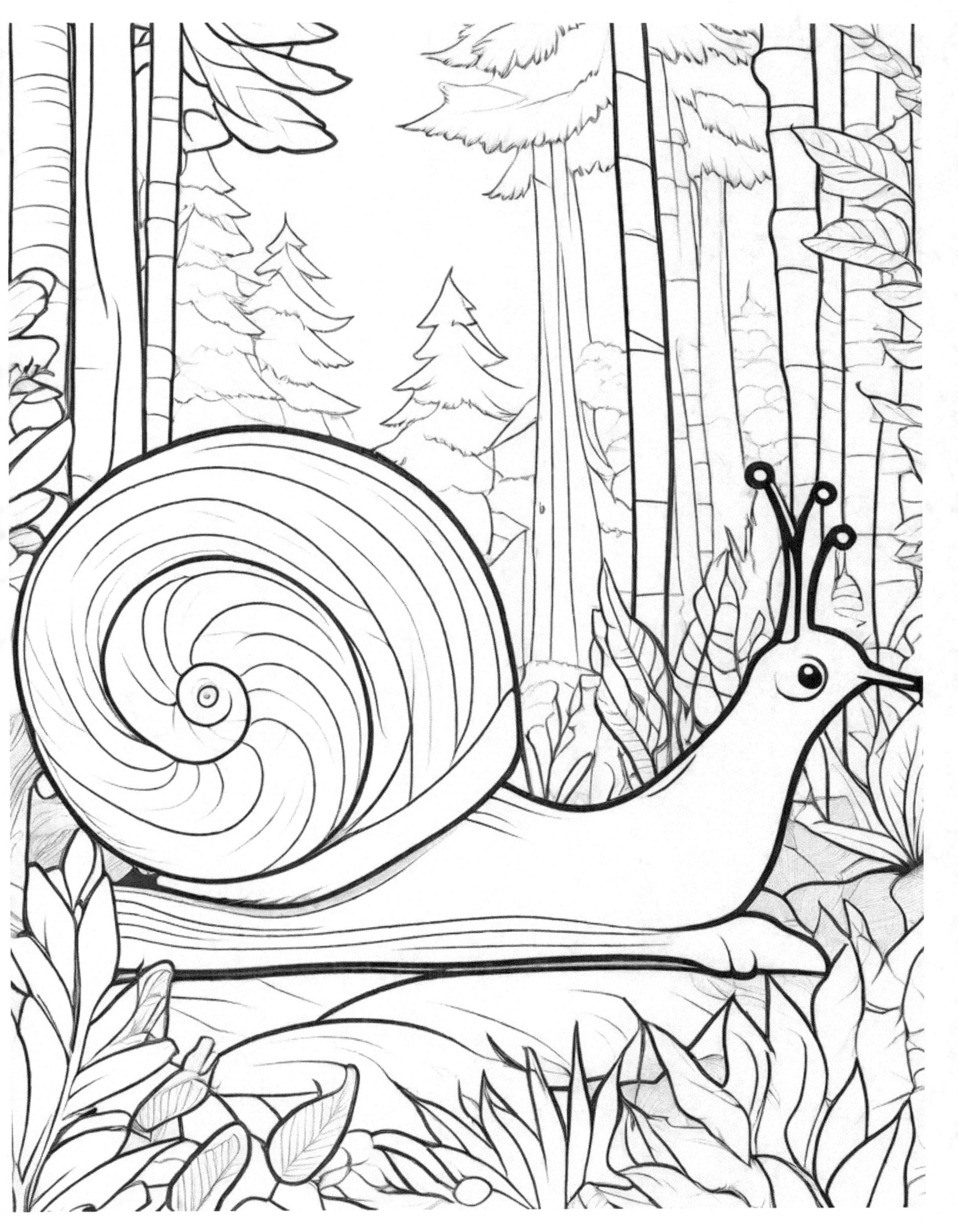

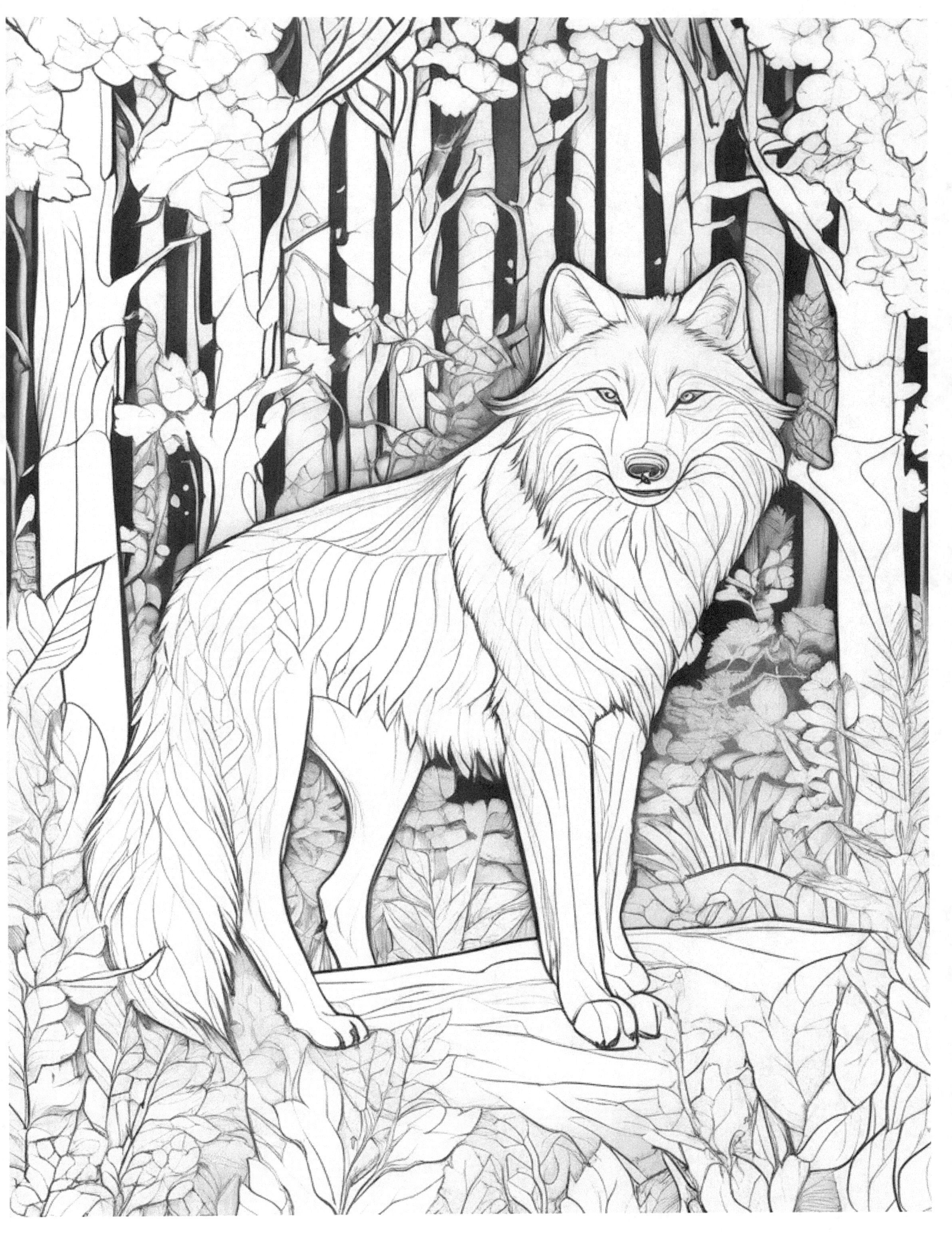

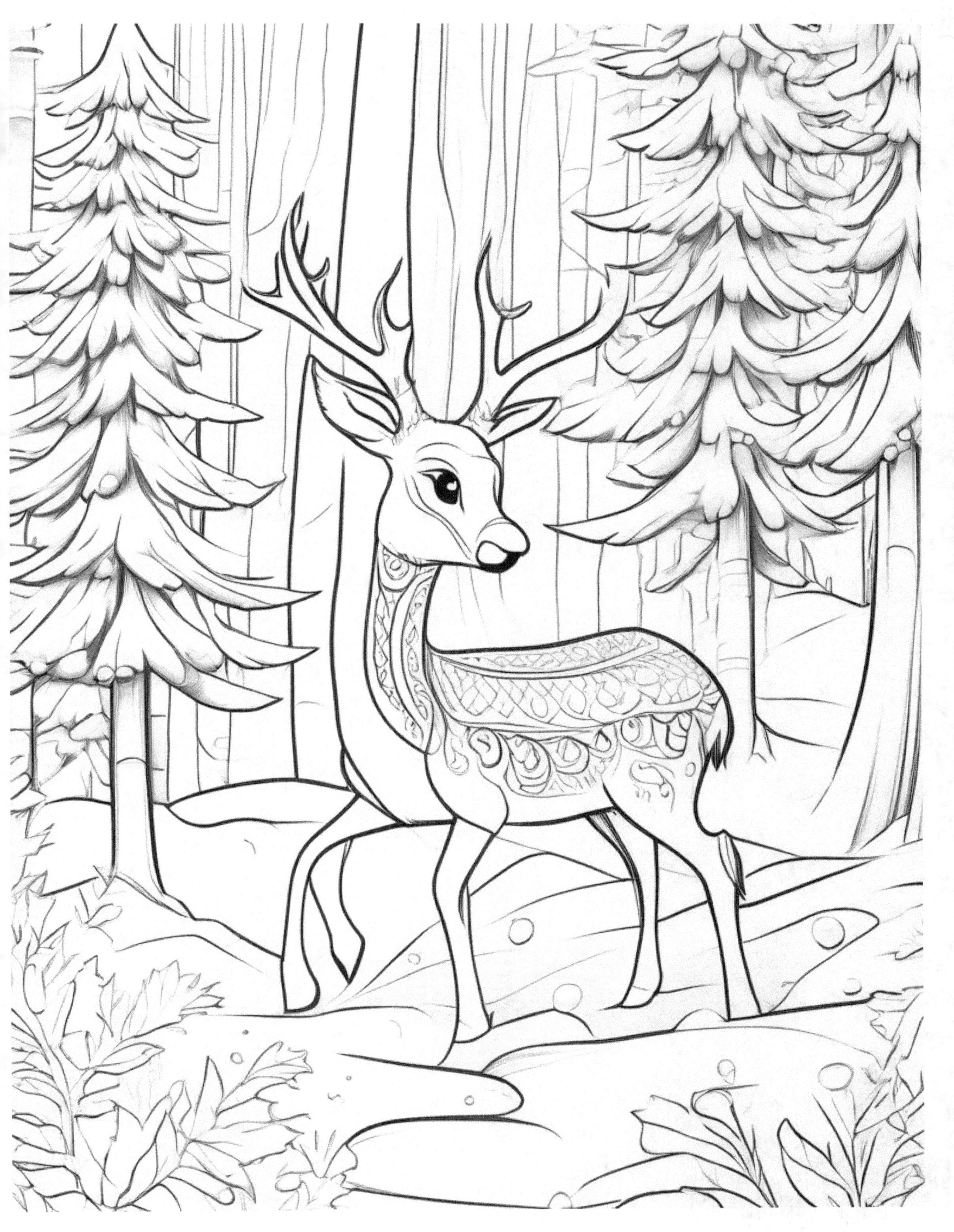

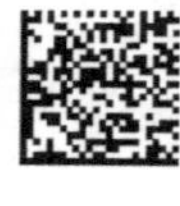